REVISE GCSE
Mathematics
PRACTICE PAPERS
Higher

THE REVISE SERIES
Available in print or online

Online editions for all titles in the Revise series are available from Autumn 2013.

Presented on our ActiveLearn platform, you can view the full book and customise it by adding notes, comments and weblinks.

Print editions

Revise GCSE Mathematics Practice Papers
Higher 9781447949886

Revise GCSE Mathematics Practice Papers
Foundation 9781447949916

Online editions

Revise GCSE Mathematics Practice Papers
Higher – ActiveBook 9781447949909

Revise GCSE Mathematics Practice Papers
Foundation – ActiveBook 9781447949930

From Autumn 2013

SOLUTION VIDEO — Worked Solution videos give step-by-step guidance on how to tackle difficult questions. They walk you through the workings, highlighting points to remember and common misconceptions. The videos offer one method of arriving at the correct answer – remember that there may be other valid methods as well.

To find out more visit:
www.pearsonschools.co.uk/mathspracticepapers

ActiveBook online edition
Revision is more than just this book!

Prepare for your exams with Worked Solution videos! These are available on the ActiveBook online edition – more information at: www.pearsonschools.co.uk/mathspracticepapers

ActiveBook is the online edition of this book: easy to use and easy to read.

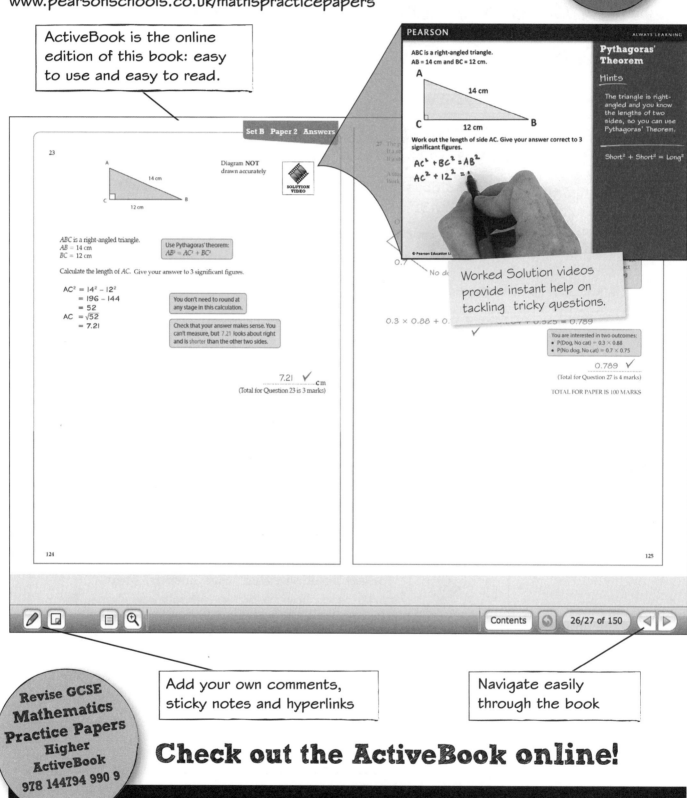

Worked Solution videos provide instant help on tackling tricky questions.

Add your own comments, sticky notes and hyperlinks

Navigate easily through the book

Check out the ActiveBook online!

Contents

Revise GCSE Mathematics Practice Papers are designed to complement your classroom and home learning, and to help prepare you for the exam. They do not include all the content and skills needed for the complete course.

A small bit of small print

Awarding Organisations publish Sample Assessment Material and the Specifications on their websites. This is the official content. The questions in this book have been written to help you practise what you have learned in your revision. Remember: the real exam questions may not look like this.

1   Here is the recipe Jackie uses for glazing her pots.

> 210 ml red
> 450 ml light yellow
> 360 ml dark yellow
> 480 ml white

(a) What volume of glazing does this recipe make?

.... ml

(1)

Jackie needs to make only 1 litre of the glazing.

(b) How much of each colour will she need?

.... ml red

.... ml light yellow

.... ml dark yellow

.... ml white

(3)

(Total for Question 1 is 4 marks)

2   Kieran wants to find out the number of text messages his classmates send.
He writes this question on a questionnaire.

> How many text messages do you send?
>
> ☐   ☐   ☐
> 10–20   20–30   30–40

(a)   Write down **two** things wrong with this question.

1 ....

   ....

2 ....

   ....

(2)

(b)   Write down a more suitable question for Kieran's questionnaire.

(2)
(Total for Question 2 is 4 marks)

3   The scatter graph shows information about some machinists making jeans.
    It shows the number of months each machinist has been working and the number of errors they
    made during the last month.

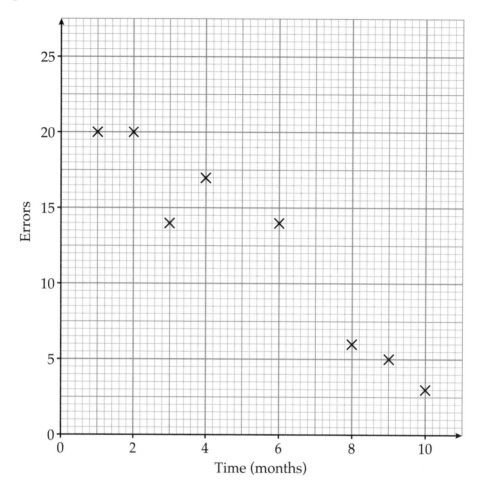

(a) What type of correlation does the scatter graph show?

....

(1)

A machinist who had been working for 7 months was also checked.

(b) Estimate the number of errors he made during the last month.

....

(2)

(Total for Question 3 is 3 marks)

4   Work out an estimate for $\dfrac{298}{0.31 \times 20.2}$

....

(Total for Question 4 is 3 marks)

5 The grid shows the straight line with equation $4x - 3y = 12$

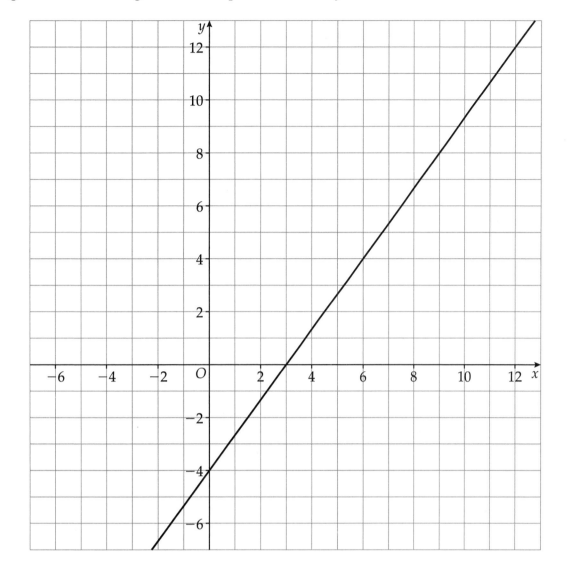

(a) On the grid, draw the line with equation $x + y = 10$

(3)

(b) Use the graph to solve the simultaneous equations

$4x - 3y = 12$
$x + y = 10$

$x =$ ....

$y =$ ....

(1)

(c) Mark with a cross (✖) any point on the grid that satisfies the simultaneous inequalities

$4x - 3y < 12$
$x + y > 10$

(1)

(Total for Question 5 is 5 marks)

6 Mr and Mrs Atkins and their two children are staying at Meadowlands in their camper van.

Meadowlands Holidays	
Camper van	£14 per night
Price per adult	£3 per night
Price per child	£2 per night

There is a 25% discount on all prices for each night after the 3rd night.

How much will it cost the Atkins family to stay 4 nights?

£.................................

(Total for Question 6 is 4 marks)

---

7 Here are the first five terms of an arithmetic sequence.

$$3 \quad 7 \quad 11 \quad 15 \quad 19$$

(a) Write down an expression for the nth term.

....

(2)

Karen says that 89 is a term of the sequence.

(b) Is she right?
Give reasons for your answer.

(2)

(Total for Question 7 is 4 marks)

8   The diagram shows a solid block of wood in the shape of a cuboid.

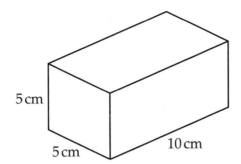

Diagram **NOT**
drawn accurately

(a)   Work out the total surface area of the cuboid.

.... cm²
(1)

Karl has to paint all 6 faces of 50 cuboids.
A can of paint covers an area of 3000 cm².

(b)   How many cans of paint must Karl buy to paint all the faces?
Show all of your working.

....
(3)
(Total for Question 8 is 4 marks)

9

A  B

The diagram shows the base of a triangle ABC.

Angle $BAC = 60°$.
Angle $ABC = 90°$.

Accurately draw triangle ABC.
Use a ruler and a pair of compasses only.
You must show all your construction lines.

(Total for Question 9 is 4 marks)

10 Given that $\dfrac{35 \times 5.4}{42} = 4.5$

work out the value of $\dfrac{350 \times 54}{4.2}$

....

(Total for Question 10 is 2 marks)

11 (a) Expand and simplify $4(9 - 2a) - 2(1 - 3a)$

....

(2)

(b) Factorise $9a^2 - b^2$

....

(2)

(c) Factorise $12p^2q + 8pq$

....

(2)

(Total for Question 11 is 6 marks)

12

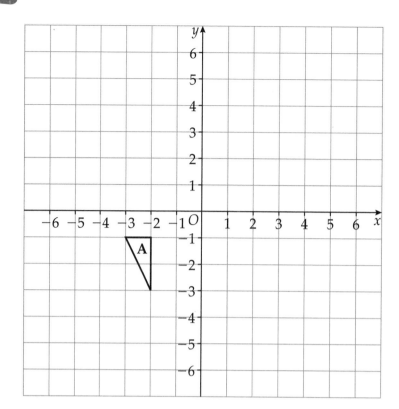

(a) Enlarge triangle **A** using a scale factor of -2 and centre $(-1, 0)$.
Label the image **B**.

(2)

(b) Reflect triangle **A** in the line $x = -1$
Label the image **C**.

(2)

(Total for Question 12 is 4 marks)

13 (a) Work out the value of $\left(\dfrac{1}{3}\right)^{-1}$

....

(1)

(b) Work out the value of $16^{\frac{3}{4}}$

....

(1)

(Total for Question 13 is 2 marks)

14 The stem and leaf diagram shows information about the number of houses in each road of the village of Garnton.

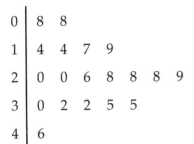

```
0 | 8  8
1 | 4  4  7  9
2 | 0  0  6  8  8  8  9
3 | 0  2  2  5  5
4 | 6
```

Key:
3 | 2 represents 32 houses

The box plot shows information about the number of houses in each road of the village of Perbury.

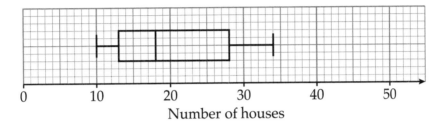

Number of houses

Compare the distributions of the two villages.

....

....

....

....

....

(Total for Question 14 is 5 marks)

15 In a Health and Safety exercise, 60 office workers were monitored for a day.
The table shows the greatest time each person spent on their computer without a break.

Time (minutes)	Frequency
$20 < t \leqslant 30$	12
$30 < t \leqslant 40$	12
$40 < t \leqslant 60$	20
$60 < t \leqslant 80$	8
$80 < t \leqslant 100$	6
$100 < t \leqslant 120$	2

(a) Complete the cumulative frequency table for this information.

Time (minutes)	Cumulative frequency
$20 < t \leqslant 30$	
$20 < t \leqslant 40$	
$20 < t \leqslant 60$	
$20 < t \leqslant 80$	
$20 < t \leqslant 100$	
$20 < t \leqslant 120$	

(1)

(Question 15 continued on next page)

(b) On the grid, draw a cumulative frequency graph for the data.

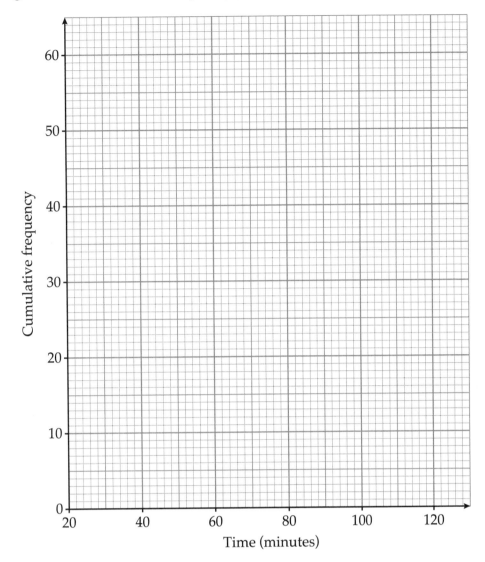

(2)

(c) Use the cumulative frequency graph to estimate the interquartile range for the data.

.... minutes

(2)

(Total for Question 15 is 5 marks)

16 (a) Write down 836 200 000 in standard form, correct to 2 significant figures.

....

(1)

(b) Work out $(7 \times 10^{-9}) \times (9 \times 10^{6})$
Write your answer in standard form.

....

(2)

(Total for Question 16 is 3 marks)

17 Work out the recurring decimal $0.5\dot{4}$ as a fraction in its simplest form.

....

(Total for Question 17 is 3 marks)

18 Saskia has a bag of balloons.

In her bag

   9 balloons are red
   3 balloons are blue
   4 balloons are yellow.

She takes one balloon from the bag at random.
She takes another balloon from the bag at random.

Work out the probability she took a red balloon and a yellow balloon.

....

(Total for Question 18 is 4 marks)

19 Make r the subject of the formula

$$V = \frac{1}{3}\pi r^2 h$$

....

(Total for Question 19 is 2 marks)

20 Here is a diagram of a parallelogram and a rectangle.

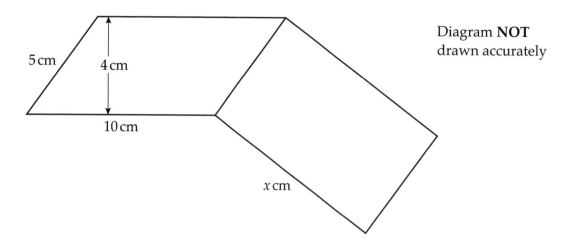

Diagram **NOT**
drawn accurately

The parallelogram has the same area as the rectangle.

Work out the length x.

.... cm

(Total for Question 20 is 3 marks)

*21

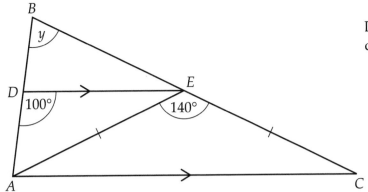

Diagram **NOT**
drawn accurately

ABC is a triangle.

DE is parallel to *AC*.
Angle *AEC* = 140°.
Angle *ADE* = 100°.
AE = *EC*.

Work out the value of *y*.
Give reasons for your answer.

(Total for Question 21 is 5 marks)

22 (a) Solve the equation $\dfrac{x}{3} - \dfrac{x}{4} = 2$

....

(2)

(b) Simplify $\left(\dfrac{4p^2q}{6pq^3}\right)^2$

....

(2)

(Total for Question 22 is 4 marks)

23 Solve the equation $3x^2 - x - 4 = 0$

....

(Total for Question 23 is 3 marks)

24

Diagram **NOT**
drawn accurately

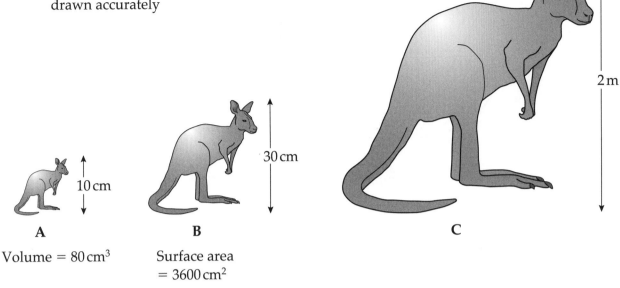

A

Volume = 80 cm³

B

Surface area
= 3600 cm²

C

2 m

30 cm

10 cm

The diagram shows three similar models from the television series *Skippy*.

Model **A** is for sale in the shops.
It has a height of 10 cm and a volume of 80 cm³.

Model **B** was used in the recording studio.
It has a height of 30 cm and a surface area of 3600 cm².

Model **C** appeared at selected cinemas.
It has a height of 2 m.

(a) Work out the surface area of model **A**.

.... cm²

(2)

(b) Work out the volume of model **C**.

.... cm³

(2)

(Total for Question 24 is 4 marks)

*25

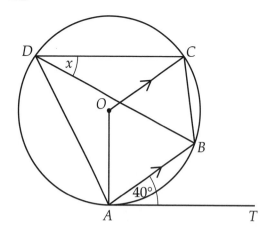

Diagram **NOT**
drawn accurately

A, B, C and *D* are points on the circumference of a circle, centre *O*.

AT is a tangent to the circle.
OC is parallel to *AB*.
The angle between the chord *AB* and the tangent *AT* is 40°.

Work out the size of angle *x*.
Give a reason for each stage of your working.

(Total for Question 25 is 5 marks)

26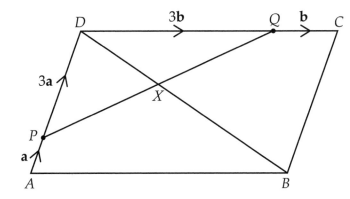

Diagram **NOT** drawn accurately

ABCD is a parallelogram.

$$\overrightarrow{AP} = \mathbf{a} \qquad \overrightarrow{PD} = 3\mathbf{a} \qquad \overrightarrow{DQ} = 3\mathbf{b} \qquad \overrightarrow{QC} = \mathbf{b}$$

X is the intersection of *BD* and *PQ*.

$DX : XB = 3 : 5$

(a) Find the vector $\overrightarrow{BD}$, in terms of **a** and **b**.

....

(1)

(b) Find the vector $\overrightarrow{PQ}$, in terms of **a** and **b**.

....

(1)

*(c) Prove that the diagonal *BD* bisects *PQ*.

(3)

(Total for Question 26 is 5 marks)

TOTAL FOR PAPER IS 100 MARKS

1 (a) Work out 15% of 60

....

(2)

(b) Write 70 g as a percentage of 2 kg.

.... %

(3)

(Total for Question 1 is 5 marks)

2

30 cm

48 cm

Diagram **NOT** drawn accurately

The top of William's games box has a rectangular shape.

He covers the top with identical square mosaic tiles.

What is the largest possible side length of tile he can use?

.... cm

(Total for Question 2 is 2 marks)

3   The table shows information about the numbers of students attending different classes at a martial arts centre.

Martial art	Frequency
Boxing	36
Tai Chi	16
Judo	48
Aikido	12
Karate	32

Complete the accurate pie chart.

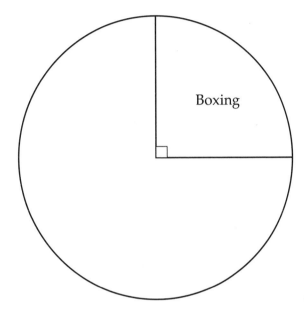

(Total for Question 3 is 3 marks)

4   The diagram shows the positions of a desert oasis O and a traveller T.

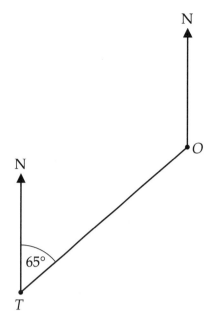

N

Diagram **NOT**
drawn accurately

(a) Write down the bearing of the oasis O from the traveller T.

.... °

(1)

(b) Work out the bearing of the traveller T from the oasis O.

.... °

(2)

(Total for Question 4 is 3 marks)

*5 Here is a diagram of a farmer's field.

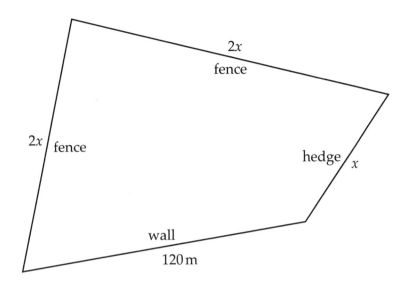

Diagram **NOT** drawn accurately

The perimeter of the field is 520 m.

The farmer wants to replace the fence with new wire.

He has 300 m of wire.
There is fencing along 2 edges.

Does the farmer have enough wire?
You must show your working.

(Total for Question 5 is 4 marks)

6 (a) Use a calculator to work out

$$\frac{174}{6.2 - \sqrt{18}}$$

Write down all the figures on your calculator display.

....

(2)

(b) Write your answer to part (a) correct to 3 significant figures.

....

(1)

(Total for Question 6 is 3 marks)

7 Two shops are selling the same jacket in the January sales.

Suits You
Jacket
£140 plus VAT @ 20%

Smarts
Jacket
£180 incl. VAT
12% off marked price

In which shop is the jacket cheaper?
Show all of your working

....

(Total for Question 7 is 5 marks)

8   (a)   The number x satisfies the inequality $3 < x \leqslant 7$

Show the inequality on the number line.

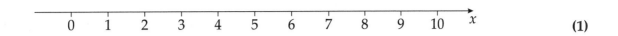

(1)

(b)   (i) Solve the inequality

$$4n + 7 \geqslant 21$$

....

(2)

n is an integer.

(ii) Write down the smallest possible value of n.

....

(1)

(Total for Question 8 is 4 marks)

9

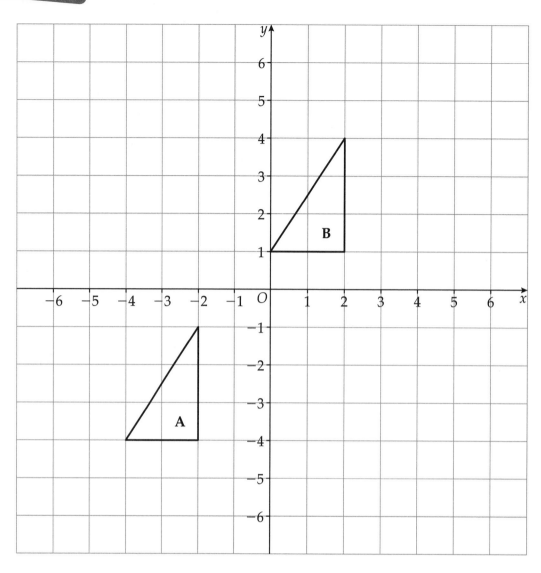

(a)   Rotate triangle **A** 90° anti-clockwise about the origin.

(2)

(b)   Fully describe the transformation that maps triangle **A** onto triangle **B**.

....

(2)

(Total for Question 9 is 4 marks)

10 The table shows the probability of the delivery of a first class letter.

Delivery time	Next day	1 day late	More than 1 day late
Probability	45x	3x	2x

Work out the probability of a first class letter arriving one day late.

....

(Total for Question 10 is 3 marks)

11   Gina invests £6000 in a bank account.
Compound interest is paid at a rate of 3.2% per annum.

Gina wants to leave the money in her account until there is at least £7000 in the account.

Work out the fewest number of years she must leave the money in her account.

.... years
(Total for Question 11 is 3 marks)

*12 The diagram shows Bridget's new sewing box and a knitting needle.

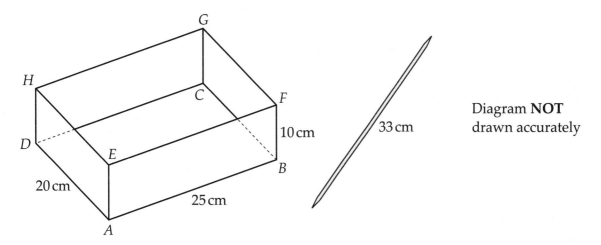

33 cm

Diagram **NOT**
drawn accurately

Will the knitting needle fit inside the box?
You must show all of your working.

(Total for Question 12 is 4 marks)

13 The diagram shows three squares.

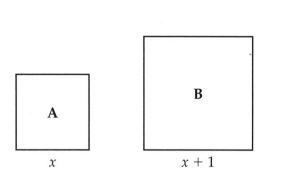

Diagram **NOT** drawn accurately

The area of square **C** is equal to the total area of squares **A** and **B**.

(a) Show that $x^2 + x = 4$

(3)

(b) Use a trial and improvement method to find the value of x.
Give your answer correct to 1 decimal place.
You must show all of your working.

$x = $ ....

(4)

(Total for Question 13 is 7 marks)

14   The table shows the services provided to the customers of a gas and electricity company.

Service	Gas only	Electricity only	Gas and electricity
Number of customers	70 000	84 000	126 000

The company wants to interview a stratified sample of 200 of its customers.

Work out the number of customers to include in the sample who receive both gas and electricity.

....

(Total for Question 14 is 2 marks)

15 Make a the subject of the formula

$$4b = m(2 - a)$$

....
(Total for Question 15 is 3 marks)

16 The amount of fruit juice bought for a function was 60 litres, to the nearest litre.

(a) Write down the lower bound for the amount of juice bought.

.... litres

(1)

The fruit juice was poured into glasses with a capacity of 200 ml, to the nearest 10 ml.

(b) Work out the minimum number of glasses which could be filled.
Give your answer to the nearest whole number.

....

(2)
(Total for Question 16 is 3 marks)

17 The diagram shows a metal rivet made by joining a hemisphere to a cylinder.

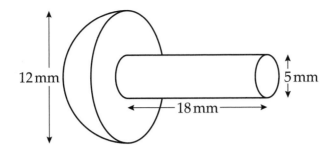

Diagram **NOT**
drawn accurately

Work out the volume of metal used to make the rivet.
Give your answer correct to 3 significant figures.

.... mm³

(Total for Question 17 is 4 marks)

18

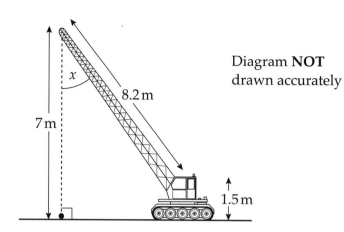

Diagram **NOT**
drawn accurately

The diagram shows a mobile crane.

Calculate the size of angle x correct to 1 decimal place.

.... °

(Total for Question 18 is 4 marks)

*19 The diagram shows a cannon ball being fired horizontally from the top of a cliff.

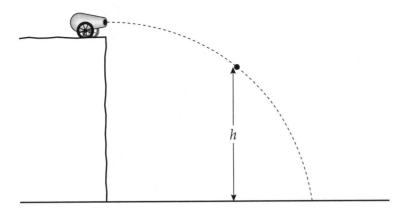

After t seconds, the height h metres of the ball is given by the equation $h = 75 - 5t^2$

Use a graphical method to estimate how long it takes for the ball to reach a height of 40 metres.

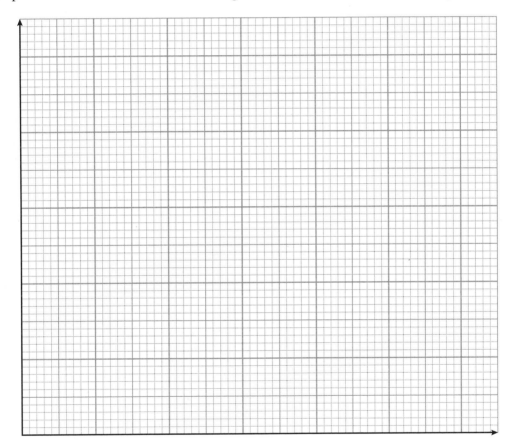

(Total for Question 19 is 5 marks)

20 The table gives some information about the heights of advertisements in a newspaper.

Height (*h* cm)	Frequency
$0 < h \leq 10$	19
$10 < h \leq 15$	17
$15 < h \leq 20$	12
$20 < h \leq 25$	7
$25 < h \leq 40$	8

One of the advertisements is chosen at random.

(a) Work out the probability that the height of the advertisement is greater than 15 cm.

....

(2)

(b) Write down the modal class.

....

(1)

(c) Work out an estimate for the mean height of an advertisement.
Give your answer to 1 decimal place.

.... cm

(4)

(Question 20 continued on next page)

(d) On the grid, draw a histogram for the information in the table.

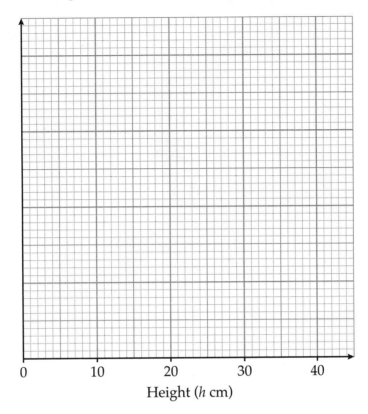

Height (*h* cm)

(3)
(Total for Question 20 is 10 marks)

21

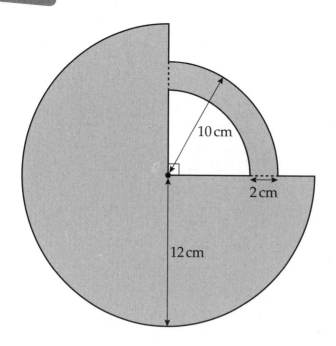

Diagram **NOT**
drawn accurately

10 cm

2 cm

12 cm

The shape is made using parts of circles.

Work out the shaded area.
Give your answer correct to 3 significant figures.

....

(Total for Question 21 is 4 marks)

22 The graph of $y = f(x)$ is shown on the grid below.
    The coordinates of the minimum point on the curve are (2, −4).

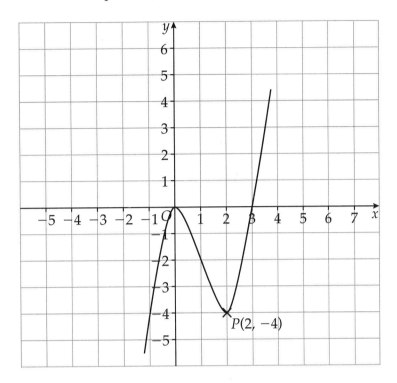

$P(2, −4)$

(a) Write down the coordinates of the minimum point of the curve with equation $f\left(\frac{1}{2}x\right)$.

    ....

    (1)

(b) On the grid, sketch the graph of $f\left(\frac{1}{2}x\right)$.

    (3)
    (Total for Question 22 is 4 marks)

23 Write $\dfrac{3x - 1}{2} - \dfrac{2x + 1}{3}$ as a single fraction in its simplest form.

....

(Total for Question 23 is 3 marks)

24 Solve $2x^2 - 8x - 3 = 0$

Give your solutions correct to 3 significant figures.

....

(Total for Question 24 is 3 marks)

25

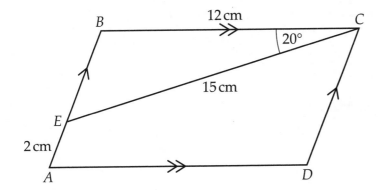

Diagram **NOT** drawn accurately

ABCD is a parallelogram.

BC = 12 cm.
EC = 15 cm.
AE = 2 cm.
Angle *ECB* = 20°.

Calculate the area of the parallelogram.
Give your answer correct to 1 decimal place.
Show all of your working.

.... cm²
(Total for Question 25 is 5 marks)

TOTAL FOR PAPER IS 100 MARKS

1   Fernando gets £20 as a birthday present.

He spends £5 on a magazine.

(a)   Express £5 as a fraction of £20
       Write your answer in its simplest form.

....
(1)

Fernando puts £3 into his savings.

(b)   Express £3 as a percentage of £20

.................................%
(2)

Fernando spends the remaining £12 on a pack of cards and some sweets.
The cards cost £2.50 more than the sweets.

(c)   How much did he spend on the sweets?

£...............................
(2)
(Total for Question 1 is 5 marks)

*2

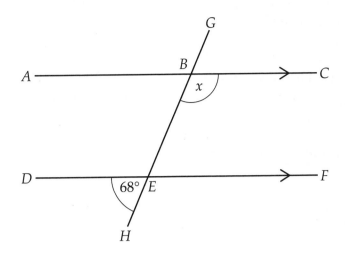

Diagram **NOT**
drawn accurately

ABC and *DEF* are parallel lines.
GBEH is a straight line.
Angle *DEH* = 68°.

Work out the size of the angle marked *x*.
Give reasons for your answer.

(Total for Question 2 is 3 marks)

*3 A fair three-sided spinner has sections labelled 1, 2 and 4
A fair four-sided dice has faces labelled 1, 2, 3 and 4

The spinner is spun and the dice is rolled at the same time.
The number the spinner lands on is added to the number shown on the dice to give
a total score.

Work out the probability that the total score is less than 5

....

(Total for Question 3 is 3 marks)

4   Femke asked 100 adults where they spent their summer holiday.
Each adult either spent their holiday in the UK or they spent their holiday abroad.

Of the 36 people who spent their holiday in the UK, 26 were men.
35 women asked spent their holiday abroad.

How many more men spent their holiday abroad than in the UK?

....
(Total for Question 4 is 4 marks)

5   Eve is the manager at a supermarket.
    She thinks that more tills must be opened because customers have to wait too long before
    being served.
    To see if this is true she records the time, in minutes, that 19 customers have to wait before
    being served.

    The table shows her results.

3.8	4.4	2.1	0.5	2.5	4.0	4.7	2.2	3.8	3.5
6.2	4.6	3.0	3.3	3.6	4.2	2.6	1.8	1.5	

   (a) Draw an ordered stem and leaf diagram for this data.

   (3)

   Eve opens more tills at the supermarket if the median waiting time is more than 3 minutes.

   (b) Does Eve open more tills?
        You must explain your answer.

   ....

   ....

   ....

   (3)

   (Total for Question 5 is 6 marks)

*6 Emir works 120 hours per month.
He is paid £8 per hour.

His rent is £400 per month.

Emir gets a pay rise of 5%.

His rent increases to £430 per month.

Is Emir better off or worse off each month?
You must show your working.

(Total for Question 6 is 5 marks)

*7

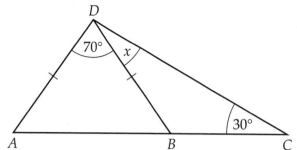

Diagram **NOT**
drawn accurately

ABC is a straight line.
BD = *AD*.
Angle *BCD* = 30°.
Angle *ADB* = 70°.

Work out the size of the angle marked *x*.
Give reasons for your answer.

(Total for Question 7 is 4 marks)

8   Solve the equation

$$3x + 2 = 7x - 8$$

....

(Total for Question 8 is 2 marks)

---

9   The diagram shows a solid prism made from plastic.
The cross section of the prism is a right-angled triangle.

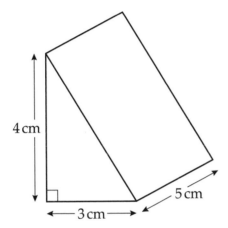

Diagram **NOT**
drawn accurately

4 cm

3 cm

5 cm

The density of the plastic is 0.5 g/cm³.

Calculate the mass of the prism.

.... grams

(Total for Question 9 is 3 marks)

10 In a restaurant, tables can be placed together for large numbers of people.

The diagram shows chairs arranged around tables.

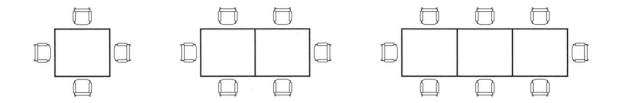

Find an expression, in terms of n, for the number of chairs at n tables.

....

(Total for Question 10 is 2 marks)

11 (a) Simplify $y^6 \div y^3$

....

(1)

(b) Simplify $3x^3 \times 4x^5$

....

(2)

(c) Write down the value of 12^0

....

(1)

(d) Work out the value of $8^{\frac{2}{3}}$

....

(2)

$3^x = \dfrac{1}{9}$

(e) Write down the value of x.

$x =$ ....

(1)

(Total for Question 11 is 7 marks)

12

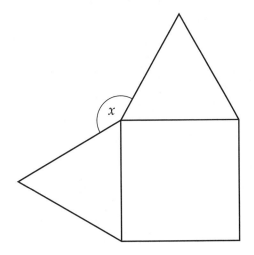

Diagram **NOT**
drawn accurately

The diagram shows a square and two equilateral triangles.

Sham says 'I could fit three more equilateral triangles around the corner of the square marked with the x.'

Explain why Sham is wrong.

....

....

....

....

(Total for Question 12 is 3 marks)

13 The diagram shows the graph of $y = x^2 + 3x - 2$

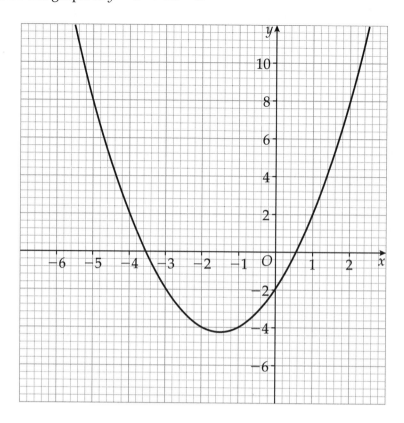

(a) Use the graph to find estimates for the solutions of

   (i) $x^2 + 3x - 2 = 0$

   ....

   (1)

   (ii) $x^2 + 3x - 2 = 6$

   ....

   (2)

(b) Can you use the graph to find estimates for the solutions of $x^2 + 3x - 2 = -6$?
   Explain your answer.

   ....

   ....

   (1)

(c) Use the graph to find estimates for the solutions of the simultaneous equations

   $y = x^2 + 3x - 2$
   $y = x - 1$

   (3)

   (Total for Question 13 is 7 marks)

14 (a) Work out the value of $(5 \times 10^4) \times (5 \times 10^5)$
Give your answer in standard form.

....

(2)

(b) Work out the value of $(5 \times 10^4) + (5 \times 10^5)$
Give your answer in standard form.

....

(2)

(Total for Question 14 is 4 marks)

15 A music download website sells singles and albums.

The music download website makes 1000 sales in one hour.
The income for this hour is £1500.

Singles cost 50p to download.
Albums cost £4.50 to download.

How many singles does the website sell in this hour?

....

(Total for Question 15 is 4 marks)

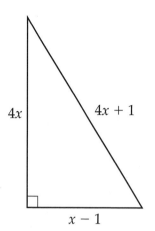

16 The diagram shows a triangle.

Diagram **NOT** drawn accurately

$4x$

$4x + 1$

$x - 1$

In the diagram, all the measurements are in centimetres.

The perimeter of the triangle is 90 cm.
The area of the triangle is A cm^2.

Work out the value of A.

$A =$ .... cm^2

(Total for Question 16 is 4 marks)

*17

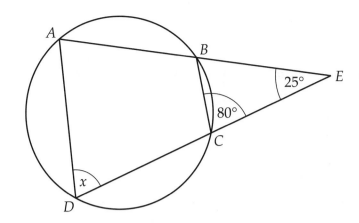

Diagram **NOT**
drawn accurately

A, *B*, *C* and *D* are four points on the circumference of a circle.

AB and *DC* are extended to meet at *E*.

Angle *BCE* = 80°.
Angle *BEC* = 25°.

Work out the size of angle *x*.
You must give reasons for your working.

(Total for Question 17 is 3 marks)

18 The cumulative frequency graph shows the amounts of time spent by students using a mobile phone to access the internet in one day.

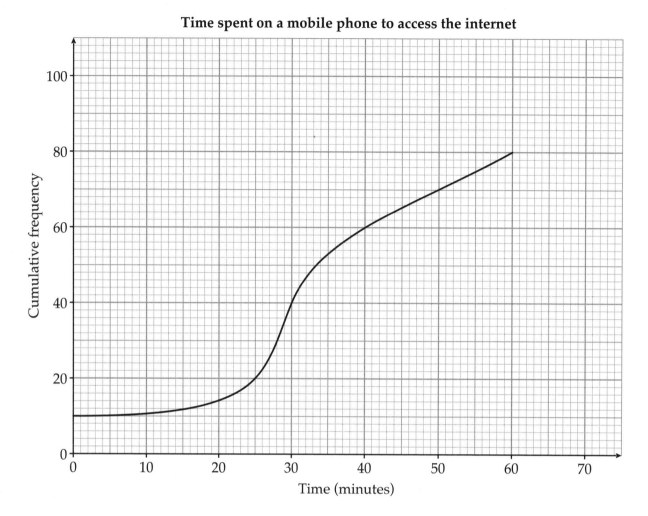

Time spent on a mobile phone to access the internet

Use the graph to estimate

(a) how many students did not use a mobile phone to access the internet

.... students

(1)

(b) the median

.... minutes

(1)

(c) the interquartile range.

.... minutes

(2)

(Total for Question 18 is 4 marks)

19 y is inversely proportional to the square of x.
   When $x = 10$, $y = 1$

   (a) Write an equation for y in terms of x.

   $y = $ ....
   (3)

   (b) Work out a value of x when $y = 400$

   $x = $ ....
   (2)
   (Total for Question 19 is 5 marks)

20   The diagram shows a quadrilateral *ABCD*.

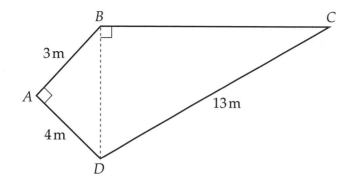

Diagram **NOT**
drawn accurately

AB = 3 m.
AD = 4 m.
CD = 13 m.
Angle *BAD* = angle *CBD* = 90°.

Calculate the length of *BC*.
You must show your working.

.... m
(Total for Question 20 is 5 marks)

21 Bag A contains six 10p coins and two 2p coins.
Bag B contains five 10p coins and three 2p coins.

A coin is taken at random from Bag A and placed in Bag B.
A coin is then taken at random from Bag B and placed in Bag A.

Calculate the probability that Bag B finishes with exactly 64p.

....
(Total for Question 21 is 3 marks)

22 Expand and simplify $(\sqrt{27} + \sqrt{3})^2$

....
(Total for Question 22 is 3 marks)

23 Three vases are mathematically similar in shape.

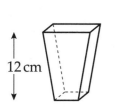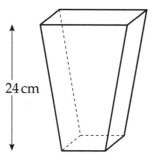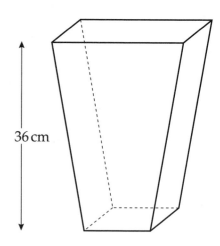

12 cm

24 cm

36 cm

Volume = 800 cm³   Surface area = 400 cm²

The smallest vase has a height of 12 cm and a volume of 800 cm³.
The medium vase has a height of 24 cm and a surface area of 400 cm².
The largest vase has a height of 36 cm.

(a) Work out the surface area of the smallest vase.

.... cm²

(2)

(b) Work out the volume of the largest vase.

.... cm³

(2)

(Total for Question 23 is 4 marks)

24 The two diagrams both show the function $y = f(x)$
Point P is a point on the function at coordinates (5, 1).

Graph A

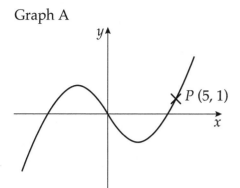

Graph B

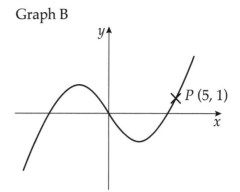

(a) (i) On graph A sketch the function $y = f(x) + 2$
     (ii) Write down the coordinates of point P after the transformation $y = f(x) + 2$

(................, ...)

(2)

(b) (i) On graph B sketch the function $y = f(x + 2)$
     (ii) Write down the coordinates of point P after the transformation $y = f(x + 2)$

(................, ...)

(2)

(Total for Question 24 is 4 marks)

---

*25 The nth term for the sequence of triangular numbers is

$$\frac{1}{2}n(n + 1)$$

Prove that the sum of two consecutive triangular numbers is a square number.

(Total for Question 25 is 3 marks)

TOTAL FOR PAPER IS 100 MARKS

1   A biased spinner has the numbers 1, 2, 3 and 4

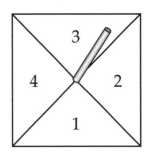

The table shows the probability of some of the numbers on the spinner.

Number	1	2	3	4
Probability	0.3	0.4		

The probability of the spinner landing on 3 is the same as the probability of the spinner landing on 4

(a) Work out the probability that the spinner lands on 4

....

(2)

The spinner is spun 120 times.

(b) Work out the likely number of times the spinner lands on 2

....

(2)

(Total for Question 1 is 4 marks)

2   Use your calculator to work out

$$\frac{\sqrt{48.3}}{3.75 \times 11.1}$$

Write down all the figures on your calculator display.

....

(Total for Question 2 is 2 marks)

*3   A supermarket sells strawberries in boxes of two different sizes.

400 g
£1.25

900 g
£2.95

Which is the better value for money?
You must show your working.

(Total for Question 3 is 3 marks)

*4   Harry works in a paint shop.
He is going to make some green paint.

He needs to mix white paint, blue paint and yellow paint in the ratio $1:4:5$ by volume.

Harry wants to make 300 litres of green paint.

Harry has
    25 litres of white paint
  125 litres of blue paint
  225 litres of yellow paint.

Does Harry have enough white paint, blue paint and yellow paint to make the green paint?

(Total for Question 4 is 4 marks)

5   The diagram shows a line segment, *AB*.

Using compasses and a straight edge, construct an angle of 30° at *A*.
You must show all construction lines.

A ————————————————— *B*

(Total for Question 5 is 3 marks)

6   The formula below can be used to work out the power produced by a wind turbine.

$$P = \frac{D^2 \times W^3}{60}$$

where
   P is the power produced in watts
   D is the diameter of the wind turbine in metres
   W is the wind speed in mph.

The world's largest wind turbine is the Siemens SWT6
It has a diameter of 150 m.

Use the formula to work out the amount of power produced by the Siemens SWT6 when the wind speed is 15 mph.
Give your answer to the nearest 1000 watts.

.... watts

(Total for Question 6 is 3 marks)

*7 The diagram shows a porch in the shape of a rectangle.

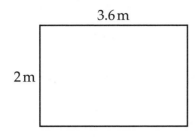

3.6 m

2 m

Diagram **NOT**
drawn accurately

The porch is 3.6 m long and 2 m wide.

Dennis is going to cover the floor of the porch with square floor tiles.

Each floor tile is a square of side 40 cm.
Dennis buys 48 of the floor tiles.

Does Dennis buy enough floor tiles to cover the floor of the porch?
You must show all your working.

(Total for Question 7 is 3 marks)

8 Carol is collecting data on photograph downloads.
   She chooses a sample of photographs and times how long they take to download.

   The frequency table shows the download times for her sample.

Download time, d (seconds)	Frequency
$0 < d \leqslant 10$	2
$10 < d \leqslant 20$	5
$20 < d \leqslant 30$	12
$30 < d \leqslant 40$	22
$40 < d \leqslant 50$	19

   (a) How many downloads did Carol complete for her survey?

   ....

   (1)

   (b) What is the modal class interval for Carol's data?

   ....

   (1)

   (c) Which class interval contains the median?

   ....

   (1)

   (d) Explain why it is not possible to calculate the exact mean of this data.

   ....

   ....

   (1)

   (Total for Question 8 is 4 marks)

9   Tony goes on holiday to Greece.

He changes £500 into euros (€) to take on holiday.
The exchange rate is £1 = €1.18

On holiday he spends €406

He changes the remaining euros back to pounds when he comes home.
The exchange rate is now £1 = €1.15

How much money does he get back?

£.................................

(Total for Question 9 is 4 marks)

10 (a) Work out the size of the angle marked x.

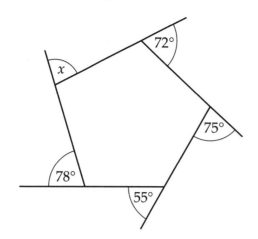

Diagram **NOT**
drawn accurately

.... °

(2)

(b) Work out the size of the interior angle of a regular polygon with 8 sides.

.... °

(2)

(Total for Question 10 is 4 marks)

11 Miss Jebson makes an artwork for the wall of her school hall.

The artwork is made from a square panel of wood.
She cuts one rectangular hole and two circular holes out of the square panel of wood.

Each circle has a diameter of 30 cm.
The rectangle is 90 cm long and 20 cm wide.

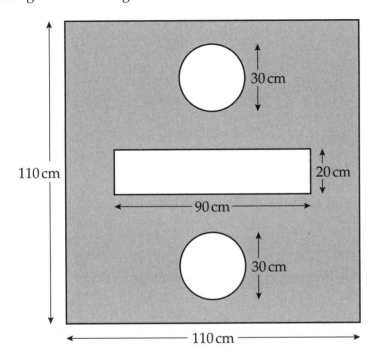

Diagram **NOT**
drawn accurately

Miss Jebson is going to paint the front of the artwork with one coat of paint.
One pot of paint covers 2500 cm².

How many pots of paint does Miss Jebson need?
You must show your working.

(Total for Question 11 is 5 marks)

12 Sam wanted to find out which holiday destinations are popular with families.
He interviewed people at Luton airport in January.

(a) His sample is biased.
Give two reasons to show his sample is biased.

1 ....

....

....

2 ....

....

....

(2)

(b) Write a suitable question Sam could use to find out which holiday destinations are popular with families.

(2)

(Total for Question 12 is 4 marks)

13 Alex walks from point *A* to point *P* on a bearing of 070°.

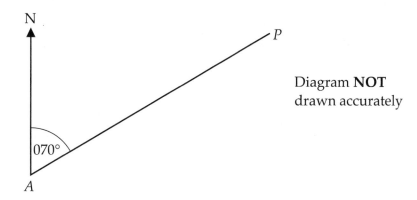

Diagram **NOT**
drawn accurately

On what bearing must Alex walk to go directly back to point *A*?

°

....

(Total for Question 13 is 2 marks)

14 A perfume house is making two new fragrances.
    Each bottle contains 350 ml.

    'Sparkle' contains cedarwood and lavender in the ratio 2 : 5
    'Shimmer' contains cedarwood and lavender in the ratio 5 : 12

    Which fragrance, Sparkle or Shimmer, has the greater amount of cedarwood?
    You must show your working.

    ....

    (Total for Question 14 is 3 marks)

15 In an experiment a spring is stretched by 27% to 32.4 cm.

    Work out the original length of the spring.
    Give your answer correct to 3 significant figures.

    .... cm

    (Total for Question 15 is 3 marks)

16   The diagram shows a solid metal square-based cuboid.

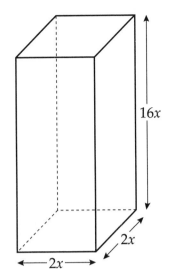

Diagram **NOT** drawn accurately

16x

2x

2x

The cuboid has a base of length $2x$ and a height of $16x$.

The cuboid is melted down and made into a cube of side length s.

Find an expression for s in terms of x.
Give your answer in its simplest form.

....

(Total for Question 16 is 3 marks)

17 Work out $\dfrac{1.8 \times 10^2}{2.4 \times 10^{-3}}$

Give your answer in standard form.

....

(Total for Question 17 is 2 marks)

18 The area of a trapezium is given by the formula

$$A = \dfrac{ah + bh}{2}$$

Rearrange this formula to make a the subject of the formula.

....

(Total for Question 18 is 3 marks)

19   A wheelchair ramp is to be built alongside 5 steps, as shown in the diagram.

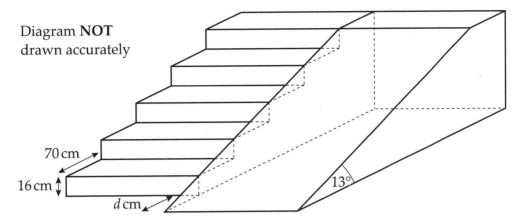

Diagram **NOT** drawn accurately

70 cm

16 cm

d cm

13°

The height of each step is 16 cm.
The depth of each step is 70 cm.
The angle of the wheelchair ramp is 13° to the horizontal.

Calculate *d*, the distance from the bottom of the step to where the ramp should start.
Give your answer correct to 1 decimal place.

.... cm
(Total for Question 19 is 5 marks)

20 Prove that the recurring decimal $0.9\dot{2}\dot{8}$ can be written as $\frac{919}{990}$

You must show your working.

(Total for Question 20 is 3 marks)

21 *ABC* is a right-angled triangle.

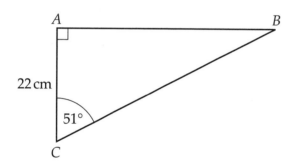

Diagram **NOT** drawn accurately

Angle *ACB* = 51°.
AC = 22 cm.

Calculate the length of *AB*.
Give your answer correct to 1 decimal place.

.... cm

(Total for Question 21 is 3 marks)

22 A factory produces vending machines that dispense cups of coffee.

Two vending machines, A and B, are tested.
Each cup of coffee should contain 250 ml of hot water.

Here is some information about the amounts of hot water contained in a sample of cups from vending machine A.

Minimum	Lower quartile	Median	Upper quartile	Maximum
248	251	254	255	262

(a) Draw a box plot to represent this information.

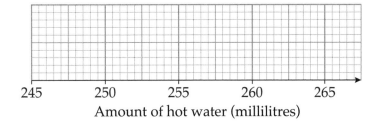

Amount of hot water (millilitres)

(2)

The box plot below shows information about a sample of cups from vending machine B.

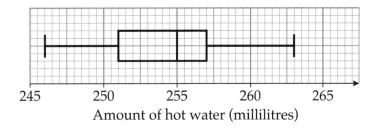

Amount of hot water (millilitres)

(b) Compare the distribution of amounts of hot water from vending machine A with the distribution of amounts of hot water from vending machine B.

....

....

....

....

....

(2)

(Total for Question 22 is 4 marks)

23 The diagram shows a farmer's field.

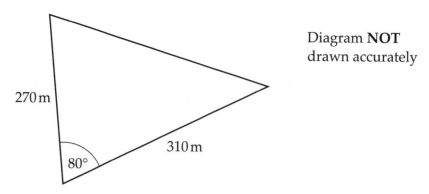

Diagram **NOT** drawn accurately

The lengths of the sides of the field have been measured to the nearest 10 m.

The farmer wants to plant grass in the field.

1 bag of seed covers 500 m², to the nearest 100 m².
The farmer has 90 bags of grass seed.

Does the farmer definitely have enough bags?
Show all your working.

(Total for Question 23 is 5 marks)

24 The table shows the heights of some seedlings.

Height of seedlings, s (cm)	Frequency
$0 < s \leq 2$	6
$2 < s \leq 4$	7
$4 < s \leq 6$	13
$6 < s \leq 9$	12
$9 < s \leq 15$	15

Draw a histogram for this data.

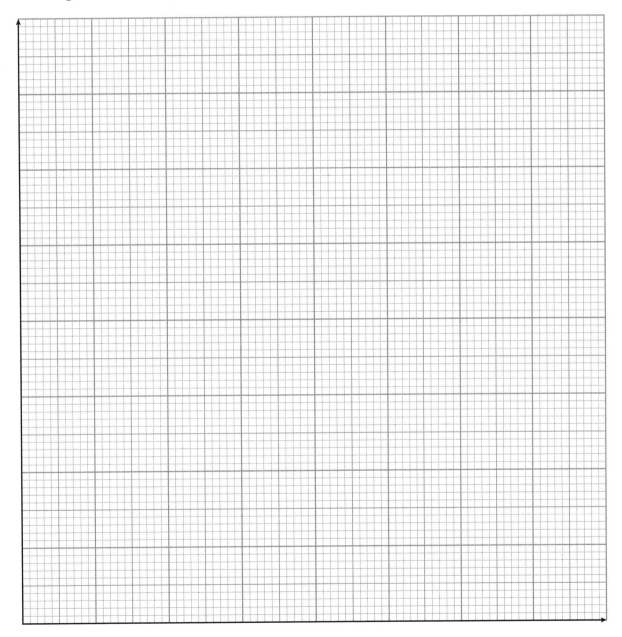

(Total for Question 24 is 3 marks)

25 A secondary school has 972 students altogether.
The table shows the number of students in each year group.

Year group	7	8	9	10	11
Number of students	198	204	214	180	176

A stratified sample of 97 students is required.

Complete the table below to show how many students from each year group should be in the sample.

Year group	7	8	9	10	11	Total
Number of students	198	204	214	180	176	972
Number in sample						

(Total for Question 25 is 3 marks)

26 Solve $3x^2 + 5x - 4 = 0$
Give your solutions correct to 3 significant figures.

....

(Total for Question 26 is 3 marks)

27

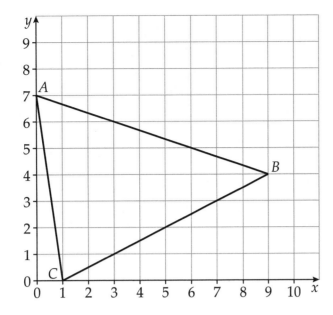

ABC is a triangle.

Work out the equation of the straight line from *C* which is perpendicular to *AB*.

(Total for Question 27 is 4 marks)

28

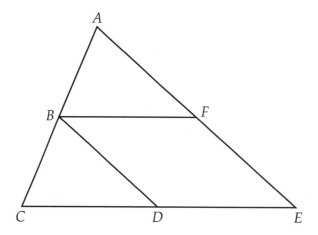

The diagram shows triangle *ACE*.

BDEF is a parallelogram where

    B is the midpoint of *AC*
    D is the midpoint of *CE*
    F is the midpoint of *AE*.

Prove that triangle *ABF* and triangle *BCD* are congruent.
You must give a reason for each stage of your proof.

(Total for Question 28 is 3 marks)

29 Work out the x-coordinates of the points of intersection of

the straight line $y = x + 4$

the circle $x^2 + y^2 = 21$

$x = \dots\dots\dots\dots\dots\dots\dots$

$x = \dots\dots\dots\dots\dots\dots\dots$
(Total for Question 29 is 5 marks)

TOTAL FOR PAPER IS 100 MARKS

1   Terri mixed 300 g of rice with 240 g of fish.

She added some onion to the mixture.

The ratio of the weight of fish to the weight of onion was 3 : 2

Work out the ratio of the weight of rice to the weight of onion.

....
(Total for Question 1 is 3 marks)

2   (a) Expand and simplify $5(m - 4) + 2(3m + 1)$

....
(2)

(b) Expand $(p - q)^2$

....
(2)

(c) Solve $5x + 2 = 3(x - 1) - 3$

....
(2)
(Total for Question 2 is 6 marks)

3   On the grid, draw the graph of $y = 2x + 3$ for values of x from -3 to 2

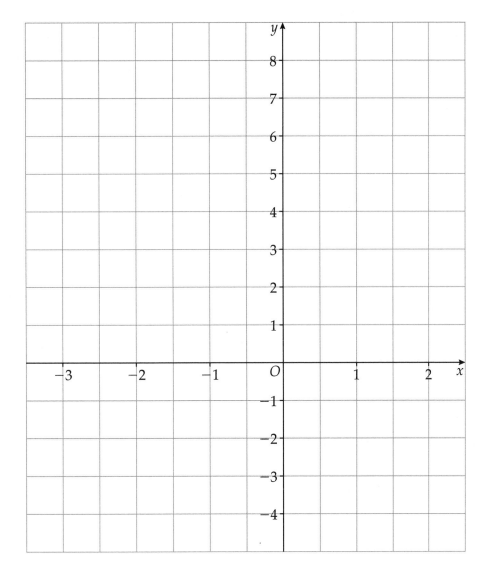

(Total for Question 3 is 3 marks)

4

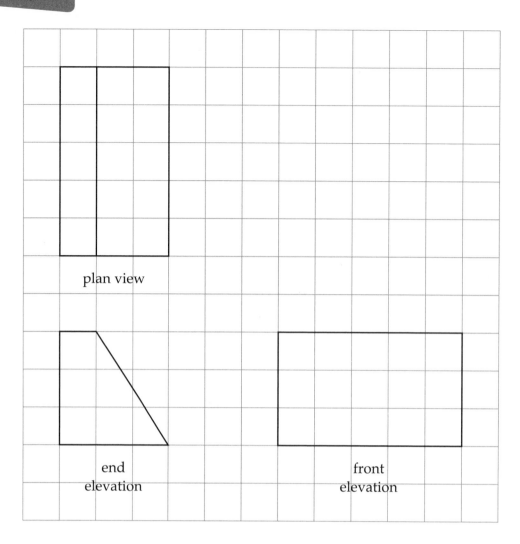

plan view

end
elevation

front
elevation

The diagram shows the plan view, end elevation and front elevation of a prism.
The diagram is drawn on a grid of centimetre squares.

Sketch the prism.
Show the dimensions on your diagram.

(Total for Question 4 is 3 marks)

5   The diagram shows an enlarged square photo inside a rectangular picture frame.

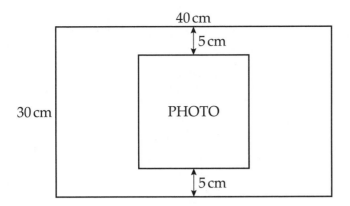

40 cm

5 cm

Diagram **NOT**
drawn accurately

30 cm

PHOTO

5 cm

The original square photo has a side length of 8 cm.

Work out the scale factor used to enlarge the photo.

....

(Total for Question 5 is 3 marks)

---

*6   Two telephone companies offer these rates for the first 12 months of a contract.

YourTel
£15 per month
Last month free

FastCom
£16 per month
15% discount for the first 6 months

Which company is cheaper for the first 12 months?

(Total for Question 6 is 4 marks)

7 The diagram shows a heptagon.

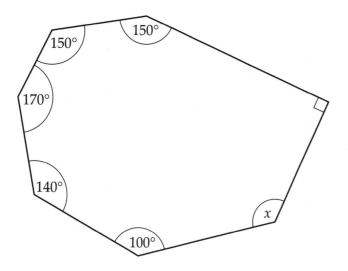

Diagram **NOT**
drawn accurately

Work out the size of angle x.

.... $^\circ$

(Total for Question 7 is 3 marks)

8   The scatter graph shows information about the numbers of people living in blocks of flats.
     It shows the number of flats in a block and the total number of people living in the block.

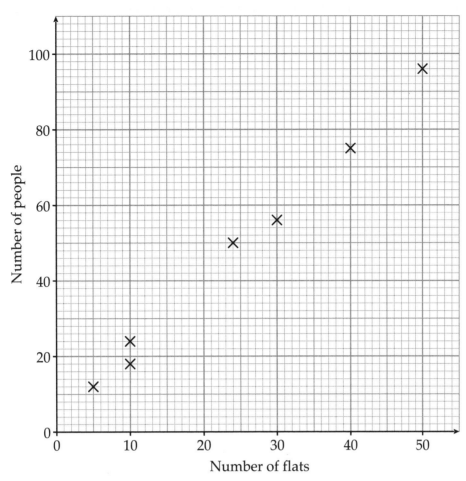

(a) What type of correlation does the scatter graph show?

     ....
                                                                              (1)

38 people live in another block of 20 flats.

(b) Plot this information on the graph.

                                                                              (1)

(c) Estimate the number of people living in a block of 36 flats.

     ....
                                                                              (2)
                                                (Total for Question 8 is 4 marks)

9   After dinner, Naim has to clear the table (C), wash up (W) or dry up (D).

She always spins this fair spinner to find out which task she will do.

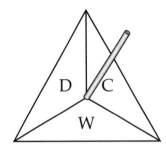

At the weekend, Naim has two dinners.

Work out the probability that she will wash up **once** at the weekend.

....

(Total for Question 9 is 3 marks)

10 Here are the first five terms of an arithmetic sequence.

    99   93   87   81   75

Marcia says that 23 is a term in this sequence.

She is wrong.
Explain why.

....

....

(Total for Question 10 is 2 marks)

11 (a) Write the number 144 as a product of its prime factors.

....

(2)

(b) Explain why $\frac{1}{144}$ is a recurring decimal.

....

....

(1)

(Total for Question 11 is 3 marks)

12 Three girls shared a full bottle of cola.

Karen drank $\frac{1}{4}$ of the bottle.

Rita drank $\frac{3}{10}$ of the bottle.

Megan drank the rest.

(a) Work out the fraction of the bottle of cola which Megan drank.

....

(3)

Rita drank 36 cl of cola.

(b) How much cola was in the full bottle?

.... cl

(2)

(Total for Question 12 is 5 marks)

*13 These two rectangles have the same perimeter.

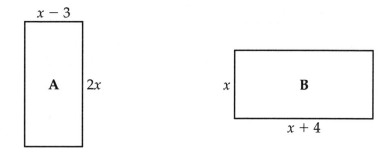

In the diagram, all of the measurements are in metres.

Work out the width and height of rectangle **A**.
Show all of your working.

(Total for Question 13 is 5 marks)

14 The diagram shows a pane of glass with a lead border.

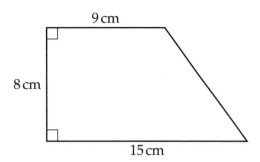

9 cm

8 cm

15 cm

Diagram **NOT**
drawn accurately

(a) Work out the area of the pane of glass.

.... cm²

(2)

(b) Work out the perimeter of the pane of glass.

.... cm

(4)

(Total for Question 14 is 6 marks)

15 (a) Find the value of $(-5)^{-2}$

....

(2)

(b) Write the reciprocal of $\sqrt{2}$ as a power of 2

....

(2)

(Total for Question 15 is 4 marks)

16 (a) Factorise $8x^2 + 2x - 3$

....

(2)

(b) Solve the inequality $-2 \leqslant 3x + 7 < 13$

....

(2)

(c) Show the solutions to the inequality on the number line below.

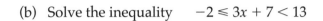

$$-8 \quad -7 \quad -6 \quad -5 \quad -4 \quad -3 \quad -2 \quad -1 \quad 0 \quad 1 \quad 2 \quad 3 \quad 4 \quad 5 \quad 6 \quad 7 \quad 8$$

(1)

(Total for Question 16 is 5 marks)

17 Solve the simultaneous equations

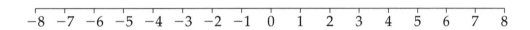

$$2x + y = 8$$
$$5x - 3y = 31$$

$x = $ ....

$y = $ ....

(Total for Question 17 is 3 marks)

18 A manufacturer tested 80 projector light bulbs to see how long they would last.
The cumulative frequency graph shows the results.

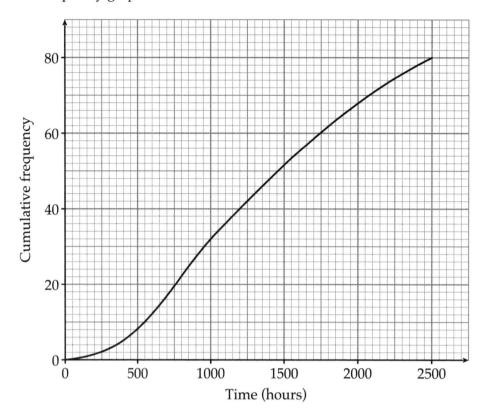

(a) Estimate the median.

.... hours

(2)

(b) Estimate the number of light bulbs that lasted more than 1800 hours.

....

(2)

(Total for Question 18 is 4 marks)

19 Solve the equation $(x + 2)^2 - 5(x + 2) = 0$

....

(Total for Question 19 is 4 marks)

---

20 Convert 0.35 m^3 to mm^3, giving your answer in standard form.

.... mm^3

(Total for Question 20 is 3 marks)

21 The speeds, in mph, of some cars were recorded as they passed a 30 mph speed limit sign.

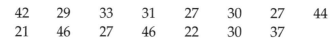

42   29   33   31   27   30   27   44
21   46   27   46   22   30   37

Draw a box plot for the data.

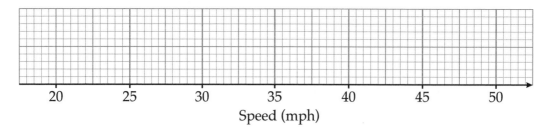

20   25   30   35   40   45   50

Speed (mph)

(Total for Question 21 is 5 marks)

22 Rationalise the denominator of $\dfrac{12 - \sqrt{6}}{\sqrt{6}}$

Simplify your answer.

....

(Total for Question 22 is 2 marks)

*23

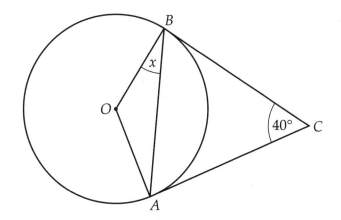

Diagram **NOT** drawn accurately

AC and *BC* are tangents to a circle, centre *O*.
Angle *ACB* = 40°.

Work out the size of angle *x*.
Give reasons for your answer.

(Total for Question 23 is 4 marks)

24 The diagram shows a kite *ABCD*.

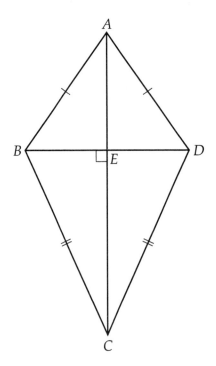

Diagram **NOT**
drawn accurately

AB = AD.
BC = DC.
Diagonals *AC* and *BD* intersect at *E*.

Prove that triangle *ABC* is congruent to triangle *ADC*.

(Total for Question 24 is 3 marks)

25 A machine makes solid plastic cylinders of different heights and radii.

The height h cm of a plastic cylinder is inversely proportional to its radius r cm.

A plastic cylinder of height 6 cm has a radius of 4 cm.

Work out the height of a plastic cylinder with a radius of 3 cm.

.... cm

(Total for Question 25 is 3 marks)

26

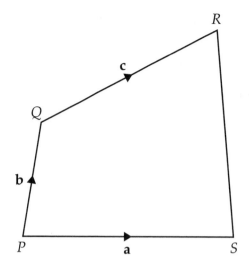

Diagram **NOT**
drawn accurately

PQRS is a quadrilateral.

$$\overrightarrow{PS} = \mathbf{a} \qquad \overrightarrow{PQ} = \mathbf{b} \qquad \overrightarrow{QR} = \mathbf{c}$$

(a) Find the vector $\overrightarrow{SR}$, in terms of **a**, **b** and **c**.

....

(1)

$$\mathbf{a} = \begin{pmatrix} 5 \\ 0 \end{pmatrix} \qquad \mathbf{b} = \begin{pmatrix} 1 \\ 3 \end{pmatrix} \qquad \mathbf{c} = \begin{pmatrix} 6 \\ 3 \end{pmatrix}$$

(b) Work out the vector $\overrightarrow{SR}$.

....

(1)

(c) What kind of quadrilateral is *PQRS*?
     Give a reason for your answer.

....

....

(2)

(Total for Question 26 is 4 marks)

27 Here are five cards.

Each card has a different single digit printed on it.
Two of the cards have been turned over.

One of the five cards is chosen at random.

The probability that it is even is 0.4
The probability that it is **not** a square number is 0.8

Work out the two numbers on the cards which have been turned over.
Show all your working.

(Total for Question 27 is 3 marks)

TOTAL FOR PAPER IS 100 MARKS

1   The diagram shows two types of plastic building block.

A

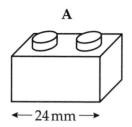

B

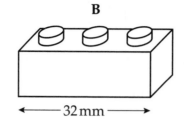

Diagram **NOT** drawn accurately

←—24 mm —→   ←——— 32 mm ———→

Block **A** is 24 mm long.
Block **B** is 32 mm long.

Jeremy joins some type **A** blocks together make a straight row.
He then joins some type **B** blocks together to make a straight row of the same length.

Write down the shortest possible length of this row.

.... mm

(Total for Question 21 is 2 marks)

2 (a) Factorise completely $15s^2t + 10st^2$

....

(2)

(b) Factorise completely $2(t - 3)^2 - 5(t - 3)$

....

(2)

(Total for Question 2 is 4 marks)

3 Alec asked a group of people how many text messages they sent yesterday.
The table shows the results.

Number	Frequency
0–4	38
5–9	24
10–14	22
15–19	15
20–24	15

Work out an estimate for the mean of the data.

....

(Total for Question 3 is 4 marks)

4   (a)   Simplify $\dfrac{12a^5}{3a^3}$

....

(2)

(b)   Simplify $(4m^3n)^3$

....

(2)

(Total for Question 4 is 4 marks)

5   (a)   Calculate $\left(4 - \sqrt{\dfrac{7.2}{5}}\right)^3$

Write down all the figures on your calculator display.

....

(2)

(b)   Write your answer to part (a) correct to 1 decimal place.

....

(1)

(Total for Question 5 is 3 marks)

6   Taahir weighs each potato in a bag.
These are his results.

200 g   221 g   184 g   199 g   223 g

190 g   190 g   186 g   206 g   219 g

186 g   205 g   206 g   192 g   198 g

(a)   Complete the stem and leaf diagram for the data.

Key:

(3)

Taahir finds another potato in the bag that weighs 220 g.

(b)   Has the range of weights changed?
Give a reason for your answer.

....

....

(1)

(Total for Question 6 is 4 marks)

7   A bowl contains 6270 ml of drink.

David fills 10 glasses with 60 ml of drink every minute.
At the same time, Rosa fills 6 glasses with 90 ml of drink every minute.

How long will it take to empty the bowl?

....

(Total for Question 7 is 3 marks)

8   A skateboard costs £42.25 plus 20% VAT.

Work out the cost of the skateboard.

£................................

(Total for Question 8 is 3 marks)

9   The equation

$$\frac{x^2}{1 + x} = 2$$

has a solution between 2 and 3

Use a trial improvement method to find this solution.
Give your answer correct to 1 decimal place.
You must show all your working.

$x = $ ....

(Total for Question 9 is 4 marks)

*10 1.25 kg of a type of cheese costs €16.55 in France.
$1\frac{1}{2}$ lb of the same cheese costs £8.97 in England.

In which country is it cheaper to buy the cheese?
Show all of your working.

1 kg = 2.2 lb
£1 = €1.15

(Total for Question 10 is 5 marks)

11 Liz stood next to her dog Jock.

She threw a stick 40 metres away from them.

Jock took 8 seconds to reach the stick, running at a constant speed.

He spent 2 seconds picking up the stick.

Jock ran back to Liz at a constant speed of 4 m/s.

(a) Use the grid below to draw a distance–time graph.

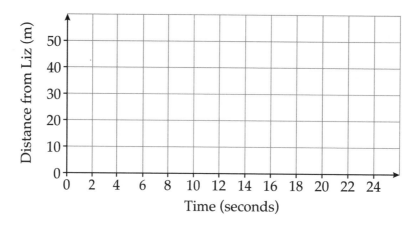

(3)

(b) Work out Jock's speed when he was running towards the stick.
Give your answer in km/h.

.... km/h

(3)

(Total for Question 11 is 6 marks)

12 A goat is tied by a rope to a railing *AB* shown in the diagram.

A ─────────────── *B*

The diagram is drawn using a scale of 1 cm to 1 m.

The rope is 3 m long.
The end of the rope can slide along the railing.

Make an accurate drawing to show the greatest area in which the goat can walk.

(Total for Question 12 is 3 marks)

13

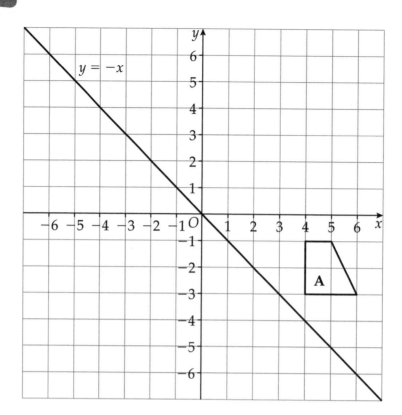

(a) Rotate shape **A** 90° anti-clockwise about the origin (0, 0).
    Label the image **B**.

(2)

(b) The line $y = -x$ is drawn on the diagram.
    Reflect the shape **B** in this line.
    Label the image **C**.

(2)

(Question 13 continued on next page)

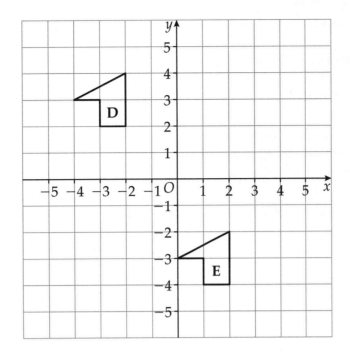

(c) Fully describe the transformation that maps shape **D** onto shape **E**.

....

....

(2)

(Total for Question 13 is 6 marks)

14 A straight line has the equation $y = 4x - 3$

(a) Write down the gradient of the line.

....

(1)

(b) Write down the equation of another straight line that is perpendicular
to the line with equation $y = 4x - 3$

....

(1)

(Total for Question 14 is 2 marks)

15 The Inland Revenue deduct tax each month from Ewan's earnings.

They base their calculations on Ewan's annual salary.

First they subtract his personal allowance of £8105 from his annual salary.
Next they calculate 20% of the remainder.
Then they divide this amount by 12 to get the amount of tax he pays each month.

Ewan pays tax of £224 each month.

Work out his annual salary.

£...................................

(Total for Question 15 is 4 marks)

---

16 The density of copper is $8.92\,g/cm^3$.
The density of silver is $10.49\,g/cm^3$.

$20\,cm^3$ of copper and $5\,cm^3$ of silver are mixed together to make a new kind of metal.

Work out the density of the new metal.

.... g/cm^3

(Total for Question 16 is 3 marks)

17 Make v the subject of the formula $T = (n + 2v)^2$

....

(Total for Question 17 is 3 marks)

---

18 $R = \dfrac{V}{I}$

$V = 2000$
$I = 5.2 \times 10^{-5}$

Work out the value of R.
Give your answer in standard form, correct to 2 significant figures.

....

(Total for Question 18 is 2 marks)

19 The diagram shows four metal ball bearings of diameter 2.7 cm packed inside
the smallest possible box in the shape of a cuboid.

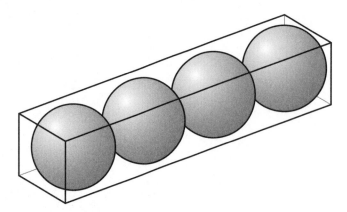

Diagram **NOT**
drawn accurately

Work out the volume of empty space inside the box.
Give your answer correct to 3 significant figures.

.... cm³

(Total for Question 19 is 4 marks)

20

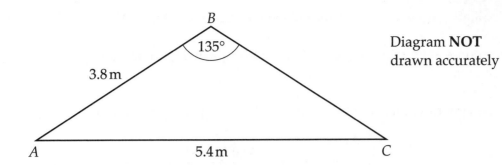

Diagram **NOT** drawn accurately

ABC is a triangle.

AC = 5.4 m.
AB = 3.8 m.
Angle *ABC* = 135°.

Calculate the length of *BC*.
Give your answer correct to 2 decimal places.

.... cm

(Total for Question 20 is 5 marks)

21 Carla is investigating how much time retired people spend watching TV.

She wants to choose a random sample of 40 retired people living in her town of Ashbury, stratified by age and gender.

The table shows information about the numbers of retired people in Ashbury.

	Age (years)		
	65–74	**75–84**	**85 and above**
Male	2000	800	400
Female	2400	1600	800

(a) How many females in the age range 75–84 should be in Carla's sample?

....

(2)

(b) Describe how Carla should choose a random sample.

....

....

(1)

Carla wants to give each person in the sample a questionnaire.

(c) Write a suitable question she could use to find out how much time they spend watching TV.

(2)

(Total for Question 21 is 5 marks)

22 Cayden weighed 60 filled shopping bags at the checkout counter of a supermarket.
   She drew this histogram for the data.

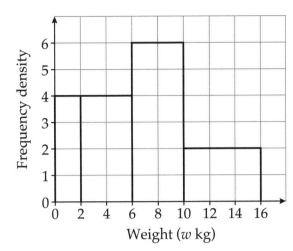

Complete the frequency table.

Weight (w kg)	Frequency
$0 < w \leqslant 2$	

(Total for Question 22 is 3 marks)

*23 Prove using algebra that the product of two odd numbers is an odd number.

(Total for Question 23 is 3 marks)

24   Solve $2x^2 - 10x + 5 = 0$
     Give your solutions correct to 3 significant figures.

(Total for Question 24 is 3 marks)

25 (a) Complete the table of values for $y = 2^x$

x	-1	0	1	2	3	4
y					8	

(2)

(b) On the grid, draw the graph of $y = 2^x$ for values of x from -1 to 4

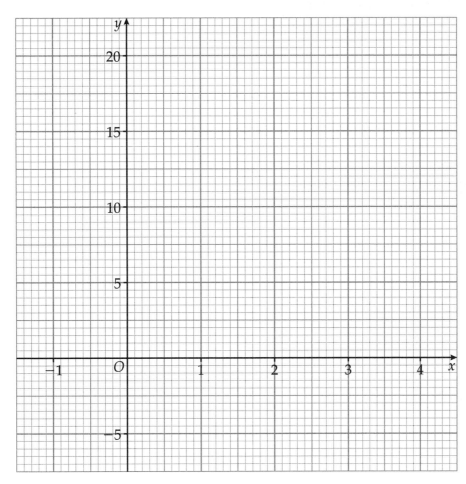

(2)

(Total for Question 25 is 4 marks)

26 The shaded part of the diagram shows a segment of a circle, centre *O*.

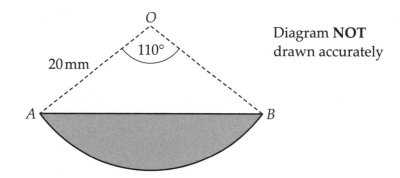

Diagram **NOT**
drawn accurately

Points *A* and *B* lie on the circumference.
Angle *AOB* = 110°.
OA = 20 mm.

Work out the area of the segment.
Give your answer to the nearest mm².

.... mm²

(Total for Question 26 is 4 marks)

27 The probability that a student at Jen's school has a dog is 0.3
If a student has a dog, the probability that they have a cat is 0.12
If a student does not have a dog, the probability that they have a cat is 0.25

A student is chosen at random.
Work out the probability that they do **not** have a cat.

....

(Total for Question 27 is 4 marks)

TOTAL FOR PAPER IS 100 MARKS

1 Here is the recipe Jackie uses for glazing her pots.

210 ml red
450 ml light yellow
360 ml dark yellow
480 ml white

(a) What volume of glazing does this recipe make?

```
  2 1 0
  4 5 0
  3 6 0
+ 4 8 0
  1 5 0 0
    1 2
```

Add together the volumes of the ingredients to find the total volume.

1500 ✓ ml
(1)

Jackie needs to make only 1 litre of the glazing.

(b) How much of each colour will she need?

Red
$210 \div 3 = 70$
$70 \times 2 = 140$ ✓

Light yellow
$450 \div 3 = 150$
$150 \times 2 = 300$

Dark yellow
$360 \div 3 = 120$
$120 \times 2 = 240$

White
$480 \div 3 = 160$
$160 \times 2 = 320$

1 litre is $\frac{2}{3}$ of 1500 ml. This means you need to multiply the amount of each ingredient by $\frac{2}{3}$.
To multiply by $\frac{2}{3}$ you divide by 3 then multiply by 2.

Check

```
  1 4 0
  3 0 0
  2 4 0
+ 3 2 0
  1 0 0 0
    1 1
```

Check that the four new quantities add up to 1 litre, or 1000 ml.

140 ml red
300 ✓ ml light yellow
240 ml dark yellow
320 ✓ ml white
(3)
(Total for Question 1 is 4 marks)

2 Kieran wants to find out the number of text messages his classmates send.
He writes this question on a questionnaire.

How many text messages do you send?
☐ 10–20 ☐ 20–30 ☐ 30–40

(a) Write down **two** things wrong with this question.

1 The ranges of the response boxes overlap. ✓

2 There is no option for people who send fewer than 10 text messages or more than 40. ✓
(2)

(b) Write down a more suitable question for Kieran's questionnaire.

How many text messages do you send each day? ✓
☐ None
☐ 1–10
☐ 11–20
☐ 21–30
☐ More than 30 ✓

Make sure that:
• your question gives a time frame
• your response boxes don't overlap
• your response boxes have options for all possible answers.

(2)
(Total for Question 2 is 4 marks)

3 The scatter graph shows information about some machinists making jeans.
It shows the number of months each machinist has been working and the number of errors they made during the last month.

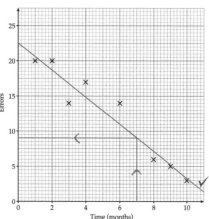

(a) What type of correlation does the scatter graph show?

Negative correlation ✓
(1)

A machinist who had been working for 7 months was also checked.

(b) Estimate the number of errors he made during the last month.

Draw a line of best fit on the scatter graph. Read up from 7 on the horizontal axis to your line of best fit, then across to the vertical axis. Your answer will depend on how you've drawn your line of best fit. An acceptable answer would be in the range of 8–11.

9 ✓
(2)
(Total for Question 3 is 3 marks)

4 Work out an estimate for $\dfrac{298}{0.31 \times 20.2}$

$298 \rightarrow 300 \quad 0.31 \rightarrow 0.3 \quad 20.2 \rightarrow 20$ ✓

$\dfrac{300}{0.3 \times 20} = \dfrac{300}{6}$ ✓

$= 50$

To estimate answers you always round each value to 1 significant figure.

Work out the bottom of the fraction first:
$0.3 \times 20 = 0.3 \times 2 \times 10 = 0.6 \times 10 = 6$

50 ✓
(Total for Question 4 is 3 marks)

5 The grid shows the straight line with equation $4x - 3y = 12$

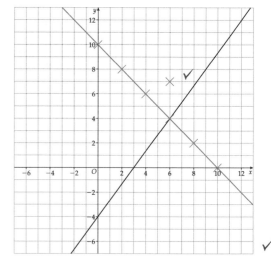

(a) On the grid, draw the line with equation $x + y = 10$

x	0	2	4	6	8	10
y	10	8	6	4	2	0
✓

You can use a table of values to draw a graph. Plot each pair of coordinates with a sharp pencil and join them using a ruler.
(3)

(b) Use the graph to solve the simultaneous equations

$4x - 3y = 12$
$x + y = 10$

The x- and y-coordinates at the point where the lines intersect are the solutions to the simultaneous equations.

$x = 6$
$y = 4$ ✓
(1)

(c) Mark with a cross (✗) any point on the grid that satisfies the simultaneous inequalities

$4x - 3y < 12$
$x + y > 10$

Check your point, for example (6, 7), satisfies both inequalities:
$4x - 3y = 4 \times 6 - 3 \times 7 = 3 < 12$ ✓
$x + y = 6 + 7 = 13 > 10$ ✓

(1)
(Total for Question 5 is 5 marks)

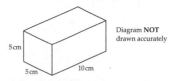
6 Mr and Mrs Atkins and their two children are staying at Meadowlands in their camper van.

Meadowlands Holidays	
Camper van	£14 per night
Price per adult	£3 per night
Price per child	£2 per night

There is a 25% discount on all prices for each night after the 3rd night.

How much will it cost the Atkins family to stay 4 nights?

<u>One night</u>
£14 + 2 × £3 + 2 × £2 = £24 ✔

> Plan your answer, and make sure you show all of your working.

<u>First 3 nights</u>
3 × £24 = £72

<u>Fourth night</u>
25% of £24 = £24 ÷ 4 = £6 ✔
£24 − £6 = £18

> 25% is the same as $\frac{1}{4}$. You can calculate 25% of an amount by dividing it by 4.

<u>All 4 nights</u>
£72 + £18 = £90 ✔

£ ....90....... ✔
(Total for Question 6 is 4 marks)

7 Here are the first five terms of an arithmetic sequence.

3   7   11   15   19
  +4 +4 +4 +4

(a) Write down an expression for the *n*th term.

Common difference = 4
Zero term = 3 − 4 = −1

> The *n*th term of an arithmetic sequence is $dn + k$ where d is the common difference, and k is the zero term.

.......$4n - 1$....... ✔
(2)

Karen says that 89 is a term of the sequence.

(b) Is she right?
Give reasons for your answer.

n	20	21	22	23
$4n - 1$	79	83	87	91	✔

> You could also write an equation:
> $4n - 1 = 89$
> $4n = 90$
> $n = 22.5$
> n must be an integer so 89 is not a term in the sequence.

No. Using $4n - 1$, 89 is not a term in the sequence. ✔

(2)
(Total for Question 7 is 4 marks)

8 The diagram shows a solid block of wood in the shape of a cuboid.

Diagram **NOT** drawn accurately

5 cm
5 cm   10 cm

(a) Work out the total surface area of the cuboid.

$2 × (5 × 5) + 2 × (5 × 10) + 2 × (5 × 10) = 250$

> There are 6 faces. Opposite faces have the same area, so you can add them in pairs.

.......250....... ✔ cm²
(1)

Karl has to paint all 6 faces of 50 cuboids.
A can of paint covers an area of 3000 cm².

(b) How many cans of paint must Karl buy to paint all the faces?
Show all of your working.

$250 × 50 = 25 × 5 × 10 × 10$ ✔
$= 12\,500$

> You could also work out:
> 12 500 ÷ 3000 = 4 remainder 500
> Karl needs to buy a whole number of cans of paint, so he needs to buy 5 cans.

4 cans of paint will cover 4 × 3000 = 12 000 cm²
5 cans of paint will cover 5 × 3000 = 15 000 cm² ✔

5 cans ✔
(3)
(Total for Question 8 is 4 marks)

9

<u>C</u>

60°
A   B

> To construct the 60° angle set the compasses to the length *AB*. With the centres at *A* and *B* draw arcs which intersect above the line. Draw a line through *A* and the point of intersection.

> To construct the 90° angle set the compasses to the length *AB*. Place the centre of the compasses on point *B* and draw an arc opposite point *A*. Continue the line *AB* to this arc. Finally construct the perpendicular bisector of the extended line.

The diagram shows the base of a triangle *ABC*.

Angle *BAC* = 60°.
Angle *ABC* = 90°.

Accurately draw triangle *ABC*.
Use a ruler and a pair of compasses only.
You must show all your construction lines.

(Total for Question 9 is 4 marks)

10 Given that $\frac{35 × 5.4}{42} = 4.5$

work out the value of $\frac{350 × 54}{4.2}$

$\frac{350 × 54}{4.2} = \frac{35 × 10 × 5.4 × 10}{42 ÷ 10} = 4.5 × 1000$ ✔

> Both numbers on top of the fraction have been multiplied by 10 and the number on the bottom of the fraction has been divided by 10. So the answer is multiplied by 1000.

.......4500....... ✔
(Total for Question 10 is 2 marks)

11 (a) Expand and simplify $4(9 - 2a) - 2(1 - 3a)$

$36 - 8a - 2 + 6a = 34 - 2a$ ✔

> Be careful with negative numbers. The final term is $-2 × (-3a)$. A negative term multiplied by a negative term gives a positive answer.

.......$34 - 2a$....... ✔
(2)

(b) Factorise $9a^2 - b^2$

$9a^2 - b^2 = (3a)^2 - b^2$
$= (3a + b)(3a - b)$

> Remember how to factorise a difference of two squares:
> $m^2 - n^2 = (m + n)(m - n)$

.......$(3a + b)(3a - b)$....... ✔
(2)

(c) Factorise $12p^2q + 8pq$

> Make sure you write the largest possible factor outside the brackets.

.......$4pq(3p + 2)$....... ✔
(2)
(Total for Question 11 is 6 marks)

12

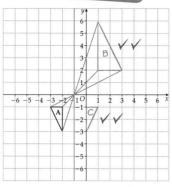

Draw lines through the centre of enlargement. The scale factor is negative so the triangle is on the opposite side of the centre of enlargement and upside down.

Draw the mirror line on the coordinate grid. The line $x = -1$ is a vertical line through $(-1, 0)$.

(a) Enlarge triangle **A** using a scale factor of -2 and centre $(-1, 0)$.
Label the image **B**.

(2)

(b) Reflect triangle **A** in the line $x = -1$
Label the image **C**.

(2)

(Total for Question 12 is 4 marks)

13 (a) Work out the value of $\left(\frac{1}{3}\right)^{-1}$

Any number raised to the power -1 is its reciprocal.

$\left(\frac{1}{3}\right)^{-1} = \frac{1}{\frac{1}{3}}$

...........3 ✓

(1)

(b) Work out the value of $16^{\frac{3}{4}}$

Use the rule $(a^m)^n = a^{mn}$ to work out the power in two stages.

$16^{\frac{3}{4}} = \left(16^{\frac{1}{4}}\right)^3 = \left(\sqrt[4]{16}\right)^3 = 2^3 = 8$

...........8 ✓

(1)

(Total for Question 13 is 2 marks)

10

---

14 The stem and leaf diagram shows information about the number of houses in each road of the village of Garnton.

0	8 8
1	4 4 7 9
2	0 0 6 8 8 8 9
3	0 2 2 5 5
4	6

Key:
3|2 represents 32 houses

The box plot shows information about the number of houses in each road of the village of Perbury.

Number of houses

Compare the distributions of the two villages.

Garnton
19 data values, so median = $\frac{19 + 1}{2}$ = 10th value
Median = 28 ✓
Range = 46 − 8 = 38 ✓

Calculate one average and one measure of spread (range or interquartile range) for each data set. Then write a sentence comparing each statistic.

Perbury
Median = 18
Range = 34 − 10 = 24 ✓

The median for Garnton is larger than the median for Perbury so on average there are more houses on each road in Garnton. ✓

The range for Garnton is larger than the range for Perbury so the data values for Garnton are more spread out. ✓

(Total for Question 14 is 5 marks)

1

---

15 In a Health and Safety exercise, 60 office workers were monitored for a day.
The table shows the greatest time each person spent on their computer without a break.

Time (minutes)	Frequency
$20 < t \leq 30$	12
$30 < t \leq 40$	12
$40 < t \leq 60$	20
$60 < t \leq 80$	8
$80 < t \leq 100$	6
$100 < t \leq 120$	2

(a) Complete the cumulative frequency table for this information.

Time (minutes)	Cumulative frequency
$20 < t \leq 30$	12
$20 < t \leq 40$	24
$20 < t \leq 60$	44
$20 < t \leq 80$	52
$20 < t \leq 100$	58
$20 < t \leq 120$	60

✓

(1)

(Question 15 continued on next page)

12

(b) On the grid, draw a cumulative frequency graph for the data.

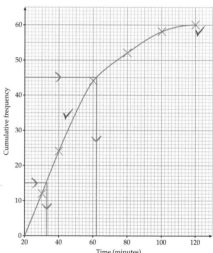

Plot the frequencies at the upper end of each class interval. Join your points with a smooth curve. Always use a sharp pencil when you are drawing graphs.

Read estimates for the lower quartile (Q_1) and the upper quartile (Q_3) off your cumulative frequency graph. Estimate for $Q_1 = \frac{n}{4}$th value. Estimate for $Q_3 = \frac{3n}{4}$th value

(2)

(c) Use the cumulative frequency graph to estimate the interquartile range for the data.

$60 \div 4 = 15$ $3 \times (60 \div 4) = 45$

Lower quartile = 33 minutes   Upper quartile = 62 minutes ✓

Interquartile range = 62 − 33 = 29 minutes

Interquartile range = $Q_3 - Q_1$

...........29 ✓ minutes

(2)

(Total for Question 15 is 5 marks)

13

16 (a) Write down 836 200 000 in standard form, correct to 2 significant figures.

> 836 200 000 = 840 000 000 to 2 s.f.

.... 8.4×10^8 ✓

(1)

(b) Work out $(7 \times 10^{-9}) \times (9 \times 10^6)$
Write your answer in standard form.

$7 \times 9 \times 10^{-9} \times 10^6 = 63 \times 10^{-3}$ ✓

$= 6.3 \times 10 \times 10^{-3}$

$= 6.3 \times 10^{-2}$

> Use the index law $a^m \times a^n = a^{m+n}$
> Remember: the number part must be greater than or equal to 1 and less than 10. Write 63 as 6.3×10 and apply the index law again.

.... 6.3×10^{-2} ✓

(2)

(Total for Question 16 is 3 marks)

17 Work out the recurring decimal $0.\dot{5}\dot{4}$ as a fraction in its simplest form.

$x = 0.5454545454...$

$100x = 54.54545454...$

$- \quad x = \quad 0.5454545454...$

$99x = 54$ ✓

$x = \dfrac{54}{99}$ ✓

$x = \dfrac{6}{11}$

> Write out more of the recurring decimal and call it x.
> Then multiply x by 100.
>
> | $100x$ | $54.54545454...$ |
> |---|---|
> | $- \quad x$ | $- \quad 0.54545454...$ |
> | $99x =$ | 54 |

.... $\dfrac{6}{11}$ ✓

(Total for Question 17 is 3 marks)

18 Saskia has a bag of balloons.

In her bag

    9 balloons are red
    3 balloons are blue
    4 balloons are yellow.

She takes one balloon from the bag at random.
She takes another balloon from the bag at random.

Work out the probability she took a red balloon and a yellow balloon.

$P(RY) = \dfrac{\cancel{9}^{3}}{\cancel{16}_{4}} \times \dfrac{\cancel{4}^{1}}{\cancel{15}_{5}} = \dfrac{3}{20}$ ✓

$P(YR) = \dfrac{\cancel{4}^{1}}{\cancel{16}_{4}} \times \dfrac{\cancel{9}^{3}}{\cancel{15}_{5}} = \dfrac{3}{20}$ ✓

$P(RY \text{ or } YR) = \dfrac{3}{20} + \dfrac{3}{20} = \dfrac{6}{20} = \dfrac{3}{10}$ ✓

> This is an example of sampling without replacement.
> On the first pick there are 16 balloons in the bag. On the second pick, there are only 15 balloons in the bag. Remember there are two successful outcomes: red then yellow, and yellow then red.

.... $\dfrac{3}{10}$ ✓

(Total for Question 18 is 4 marks)

19 Make r the subject of the formula

$$V = \frac{1}{3}\pi r^2 h$$

$3V = \pi r^2 h$

$r^2 = \dfrac{3V}{\pi h}$ ✓

$r = \sqrt{\dfrac{3V}{\pi h}}$

> Follow these steps to get r on its own on one side of the formula:
> • multiply everything by 3
> • divide everything by πh
> • take square roots of both sides of the equation.

.... $r = \sqrt{\dfrac{3V}{\pi h}}$ ✓

(Total for Question 19 is 2 marks)

20 Here is a diagram of a parallelogram and a rectangle.

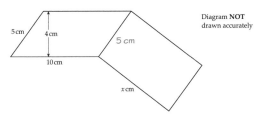

Diagram **NOT** drawn accurately

The parallelogram has the same area as the rectangle.

Work out the length x.

Area of parallelogram $= 10 \times 4 = 40 \text{ cm}^2$ ✓

Area of rectangle $= 5 \times x$

> Area of a parallelogram = base × vertical height
> You need to remember this formula – it's not given on the formula sheet

$5x = 40$

$x = 8$ ✓

.... 8 ✓ cm

(Total for Question 20 is 3 marks)

*21

Diagram **NOT** drawn accurately

ABC is a triangle.

DE is parallel to AC.
Angle $AEC = 140°$.
Angle $ADE = 100°$.
$AE = EC$.

Work out the value of y.
Give reasons for your answer.

EAC is an isosceles triangle.

$\angle EAC = \angle ECA = (180° - 140°) \div 2 = 40° \div 2 = 20°$ ✓

Base angles of an isosceles triangle are equal.

$\angle BED = 20°$ ✓

Corresponding angles on parallel lines are equal.

$y = 100° - 20° = 80°$ ✓

Exterior angle of a triangle equals sum of two opposite interior angles. ✓

> There is more than one way to answer this question. Make sure that you give a reason for each step of your working, and write any angles you have worked out on the diagram. Some of the other reasons you could use to answer this question are:
> • angles on a straight line add up to 180°
> • angles in a triangle add up to 180°
> • alternate angles on parallel lines are equal
> • allied (supplementary) angles on parallel lines add up to 180°.

(Total for Question 21 is 5 marks)

22 (a) Solve the equation $\frac{x}{3} - \frac{x}{4} = 2$

$$4\cancel{12}\left(\frac{x}{\cancel{3}}\right) - 3\cancel{12}\left(\frac{x}{\cancel{4}}\right) = 24$$

$$4x - 3x = 24 \checkmark$$

$$x = 24$$

> Start by getting rid of the fractions.
> Multiply both sides of the equation by the lowest common multiple of the two denominators.
> The lowest common multiple of 3 and 4 is 12.

$$x = 24 \checkmark$$
(2)

(b) Simplify $\left(\frac{4p^2q}{6pq^3}\right)^2$

$$\left(\frac{\cancel{4}^2 \cancel{p^2} \cancel{q}}{\cancel{6}_3 \cancel{p} \cancel{q^3}^2}\right)^2 = \left(\frac{2p}{3q^2}\right)^2 = \frac{4p^2}{9q^4}$$

> Simplify the expression inside the brackets by cancelling common factors on the top and bottom of the fraction.
> Then square the numerator and square the denominator.

$$\frac{4p^2}{9q^4} \checkmark \checkmark$$
(2)

(Total for Question 22 is 4 marks)

23 Solve the equation $3x^2 - x - 4 = 0$

$$(3x - 4)(x + 1) = 0 \checkmark$$

$$3x - 4 = 0 \quad \text{or} \quad x + 1 = 0$$

$$x = \frac{4}{3} \checkmark \qquad x = -1$$

> This is a non-calculator paper, so don't try to use the quadratic formula. You need to factorise the left-hand side of the equation. The factorised expression will look like $(3x \pm \square)(x \pm \square)$

$$x = \frac{4}{3} \text{ or } x = -1 \checkmark$$

(Total for Question 23 is 3 marks)

24

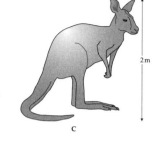
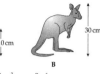

Diagram NOT drawn accurately

A — 10 cm — Volume = 80 cm³

B — 30 cm — Surface area = 3600 cm²

C — 2 m

The diagram shows three similar models from the television series *Skippy*.

Model **A** is for sale in the shops.
It has a height of 10 cm and a volume of 80 cm³.

Model **B** was used in the recording studio.
It has a height of 30 cm and a surface area of 3600 cm².

Model **C** appeared at selected cinemas.
It has a height of 2 m.

(a) Work out the surface area of model **A**.

$$k = 30 \div 10 = 3$$
$$k^2 = 3^2 = 9 \checkmark$$
$$3600 \div 9 = 400$$

> Work out the scale factor for length from model **A** to model **B**. Write this as k.
> The scale factor for surface area will be k^2.

$$400 \checkmark \text{ cm}^2$$
(2)

(b) Work out the volume of model **C**.

$$k = 200 \div 10 = 20$$
$$k^3 = 20^3 = 20 \times 400 = 8000 \checkmark$$
$$80 \times 8000 = 640\,000$$

> Work out the scale factor for length from model **A** to model **C**. Write this as k.
> The scale factor for volume will be k^3.

> Check that your answers make sense.
> **A** is smaller than **B** so it will have a smaller surface area.
> **C** is larger than **A** so it will have a larger volume.

$$640\,000 \checkmark \text{ cm}^3$$
(2)

(Total for Question 24 is 4 marks)

---

*25

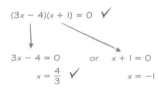

Diagram NOT drawn accurately

A, B, C and D are points on the circumference of a circle, centre O.

AT is a tangent to the circle.
OC is parallel to AB.
The angle between the chord AB and the tangent AT is 40°.

Work out the size of angle x.
Give a reason for each stage of your working.

$$\angle BAO = 90° - 40° = 50°$$

Angle between a tangent and a radius is 90°. $\checkmark$

> Write any angles you work out on the diagram, and remember to give reasons for each step of your working.

$$\angle AOC = 180° - 50° = 130°$$

Allied (supplementary) angles on parallel lines. $\checkmark$

$$\angle ADC = 130° \div 2 = 65°$$

Angle subtended at the centre is twice the angle subtended at the circumference. $\checkmark$

$$\angle ADB = 40°$$

Alternate segment theorem $\checkmark$

> The alternate segment theorem says that the angle between a tangent (XZ) and a chord (VY) is equal to the angle in the opposite segment:
>
>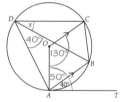
>
> $\angle XYV = \angle VWY$

$$x = 65° - 40° = 25° \checkmark$$

(Total for Question 25 is 5 marks)

26

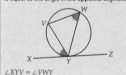

Diagram NOT drawn accurately

$ABCD$ is a parallelogram.

$$\overrightarrow{AP} = \mathbf{a} \qquad \overrightarrow{PD} = 3\mathbf{a} \qquad \overrightarrow{DQ} = 3\mathbf{b} \qquad \overrightarrow{QC} = \mathbf{b}$$

X is the intersection of BD and PQ.
$DX : XB = 3 : 5$

(a) Find the vector $\overrightarrow{BD}$, in terms of $\mathbf{a}$ and $\mathbf{b}$.

$$\overrightarrow{BD} = \overrightarrow{BC} + \overrightarrow{CD} = 4\underline{a} - 4\underline{b}$$

> $ABCD$ is a parallelogram, so $\overrightarrow{BC} = \overrightarrow{AD}$.

$$4\underline{a} - 4\underline{b} \checkmark$$
(1)

(b) Find the vector $\overrightarrow{PQ}$, in terms of $\mathbf{a}$ and $\mathbf{b}$.

> Follow a path around the shape to get from P to Q.

$$\overrightarrow{PQ} = \overrightarrow{PD} + \overrightarrow{DQ} = 3\underline{a} + 3\underline{b}$$

$$3\underline{a} + 3\underline{b} \checkmark$$
(1)

*(c) Prove that the diagonal BD bisects PQ.

$$\overrightarrow{PX} = \overrightarrow{PD} + \overrightarrow{DX} = 3\underline{a} + \frac{3}{8}\overrightarrow{DB} = 3\underline{a} + \frac{3}{8}(-\overrightarrow{BD}) = 3\underline{a} + \frac{3}{8}(-4\underline{a} + 4\underline{b})$$
$$\checkmark$$

> The ratio $DX : XB = 3 : 5$ so $\overrightarrow{DX} = \frac{3}{8}\overrightarrow{DB}$.

$$= 3\underline{a} - \frac{12}{8}\underline{a} + \frac{12}{8}\underline{b}$$

> You can use your answer to part (a) in your proof.

$$= 3\underline{a} - \frac{3}{2}\underline{a} + \frac{3}{2}\underline{b}$$
$$= \frac{3}{2}\underline{a} + \frac{3}{2}\underline{b}$$

$$\overrightarrow{XQ} = \overrightarrow{XD} + \overrightarrow{DQ} = \frac{3}{8}\overrightarrow{BD} + 3\underline{b} = \frac{3}{8}(4\underline{a} - 4\underline{b}) + 3\underline{b}$$
$$= \frac{3}{2}\underline{a} - \frac{3}{2}\underline{b} + 3\underline{b}$$
$$= \frac{3}{2}\underline{a} + \frac{3}{2}\underline{b} \checkmark$$

So $\overrightarrow{PX} = \overrightarrow{XQ}$. X is the midpoint of PQ, so BD bisects PQ. $\checkmark$
(3)

> State what you have proved at the end of your proof.

(Total for Question 26 is 5 marks)

TOTAL FOR PAPER IS 100 MARKS

1 (a) Work out 15% of 60

$60 \times \dfrac{15}{100} = 9$ ✓

15% = $\frac{15}{100}$ = 0.15.
You can calculate 15% of an amount by multiplying by $\frac{15}{100}$ or by multiplying by 0.15.

.... 9 ✓
(2)

(b) Write 70 g as a percentage of 2 kg.

Make sure both quantities are in the same units.
2 kg = 2000 g.
Write one quantity as a fraction of the other, then multiply by 100 to convert the fraction into a percentage.

$2 \times 1000 = 2000$ ✓

$\dfrac{70}{2000} \times 100 = 3.5$

✓

.... 3.5 ✓ %
(3)
(Total for Question 1 is 5 marks)

2

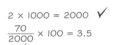

30 cm

48 cm

Diagram **NOT** drawn accurately

The top of William's games box has a rectangular shape.

He covers the top with identical square mosaic tiles.

What is the largest possible side length of tile he can use?

Factors of 30: 1, 2, 3, 5, ⑥, 10, 15, 30
Factors of 48: 1, 2, 3, 4, ⑥, 8, 12, 16, 24, 48 ✓

Find the highest common factor of 30 and 48. This is the largest tile which will fit exactly along both sides of the rectangle.

.... 6 ✓ cm
(Total for Question 2 is 2 marks)

---

3 The table shows information about the numbers of students attending different classes at a martial arts centre.

Martial art	Frequency	Sector angle
Boxing	36	36 × 2.5 = 90
Tai Chi	16	16 × 2.5 = 40 ✓
Judo	48	48 × 2.5 = 120
Aikido	12	12 × 2.5 = 30
Karate	32	32 × 2.5 = 80

Add a column to the table for sector angle.

Complete the accurate pie chart.

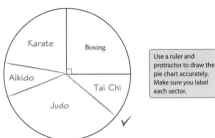

Karate Boxing

Aikido

Tai Chi

Judo

✓

Use a ruler and protractor to draw the pie chart accurately. Make sure you label each sector.

$36 + 16 + 48 + 12 + 32 = 144$
$360 \div 144 = 2.5$ ✓

Divide 360° by the total frequency to work out the angle that represents one person. Each person = 2.5°, so multiply each frequency by 2.5° to work out the angle of each sector.

<u>Check</u>
$90 + 40 + 120 + 30 + 80 = 360$

It's a good idea to check that all your sector angles add up to 360°.

(Total for Question 3 is 3 marks)

---

4 The diagram shows the positions of a desert oasis O and a traveller T.

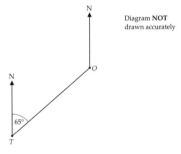

N

N

65°

O

T

Diagram **NOT** drawn accurately

(a) Write down the bearing of the oasis O from the traveller T.

Remember that bearings always have three figures.

.... 065 ✓ °
(1)

(b) Work out the bearing of the traveller T from the oasis O.

✓

$65 + 180 = 245$

To find a reverse bearing add or subtract 180°.

.... 245 ✓ °
(2)
(Total for Question 4 is 3 marks)

---

*5 Here is a diagram of a farmer's field.

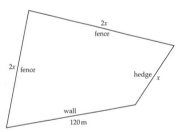

2x fence

2x fence

hedge

x

wall
120 m

Diagram **NOT** drawn accurately

The perimeter of the field is 520 m.

The farmer wants to replace the fence with new wire.

He has 300 m of wire.
There is fencing along 2 edges.

Does the farmer have enough wire?
You must show your working.

$2x + 2x + x + 120 = 520$ ✓
$5x + 120 = 520$
$5x = 400$
$x = 80$ ✓

Use the information in the question to write an equation. Solve your equation to find x.

$2x + 2x = 4x$
$= 4 \times 80$
$= 320$ ✓

Work out the length of the fence, and compare this to the amount of wire the farmer has. Make sure you show all your working and answer the question 'yes' or 'no'.

No. The farmer needs 320 m of wire and only has 300 m. ✓

(Total for Question 5 is 4 marks)

6 (a) Use a calculator to work out

$$\frac{174}{6.2 - \sqrt{18}}$$

> Show what the bottom of the fraction comes to in your working. You can check your answer by entering it into the calculator in one go.

Write down all the figures on your calculator display.

174 ÷ 1.957 359 313 ✓   88.89527786 ✓

....

(2)

(b) Write your answer to part (a) correct to 3 significant figures.

88.9 ✓

....

(1)

(Total for Question 6 is 3 marks)

7 Two shops are selling the same jacket in the January sales.

> **Suits You**
> Jacket
> £140 plus VAT @ 20%

> **Smarts**
> Jacket
> £180 incl. VAT
> 12% off marked price

In which shop is the jacket cheaper?
Show all of your working

Suits You

$$\frac{20}{100} \times 140 = 28 \text{ ✓}$$

140 + 28 = 168 ✓

> Increase £140 by 20% and reduce £180 by 12%, then compare the answers.
> You could also use multipliers:
> • the multiplier for a 20% increase is 1.2
> • the multiplier for a 12% decrease is 0.88.

Smarts

$$\frac{12}{100} \times 180 = 21.6 \text{ ✓}$$

180 − 21.6 = 158.4 ✓

> Make sure you answer the question by writing down which shop is cheaper.

Smarts ✓

....

(Total for Question 7 is 5 marks)

8 (a) The number x satisfies the inequality $3 < x \leqslant 7$

Show the inequality on the number line.

> Use a closed circle for ⩽ or ⩾ and an open circle for < or >

(1)

(b) (i) Solve the inequality

$$4n + 7 \geqslant 21$$

$$4n + 7 \geqslant 21$$
$$4n \geqslant 14 \text{ ✓}$$
$$n \geqslant 3.5$$

> Your answer should have the letter on its own on one side of the inequality and a number on the other side.

$$n \geqslant 3.5 \text{ ✓}$$

....

(2)

n is an integer.

(ii) Write down the smallest possible value of n.

4 ✓

....

(1)

(Total for Question 8 is 4 marks)

9

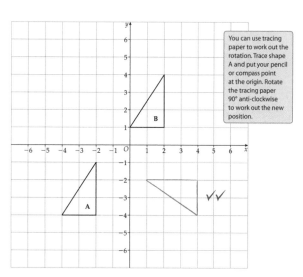

(a) Rotate triangle **A** 90° anti-clockwise about the origin.

> You can use tracing paper to work out the rotation. Trace shape A and put your pencil or compass point at the origin. Rotate the tracing paper 90° anti-clockwise to work out the new position.

(2)

(b) Fully describe the transformation that maps triangle **A** onto triangle **B**.

Translation ✓ by $\begin{pmatrix} 4 \\ 5 \end{pmatrix}$ ✓

....

(2)

(Total for Question 9 is 4 marks)

> You must use a vector to describe a translation. The top number describes the horizontal movement and the bottom number describes the vertical movement.
> • Positive numbers: movement right or up.
> • Negative numbers: movement left or down.

10 The table shows the probability of the delivery of a first class letter.

Delivery time	Next day	1 day late	More than 1 day late
Probability	$45x$	$3x$	$2x$

Work out the probability of a first class letter arriving one day late.

$$45x + 3x + 2x = 1 \text{ ✓}$$
$$50x = 1$$
$$x = \frac{1}{50} \text{ ✓}$$
$$3x = \frac{3}{50}$$

> The probabilities of all the mutually exclusive outcomes of an event add up to 1. Use this information to form an equation and solve it to work out x.

> You can give probabilities as decimals or as fractions: $\frac{3}{50} = 0.06$.

$$\frac{3}{50} \text{ ✓}$$

....

(Total for Question 10 is 3 marks)

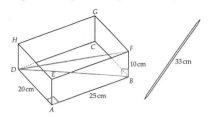

11 Gina invests £6000 in a bank account.
Compound interest is paid at a rate of 3.2% per annum.

Gina wants to leave the money in her account until there is at least £7000 in the account.

Work out the fewest number of years she must leave the money in her account.

$100 + 3.2 = 103.2$

$\dfrac{103.2}{100} = 1.032$

> The multiplier for a 3.2% increase is 1.032.
> Use the formula for compound interest to work out the amount in Gina's account after each year:
> Amount after n years = starting amount × multiplier^n

$6000 \times 1.032 = 6192$ ✓
$6000 \times 1.032^2 = 6390.144$
$6000 \times 1.032^3 = 6594.6286...$
$6000 \times 1.032^4 = 6805.6567...$
$6000 \times 1.032^5 = 7023.4377...$ ✓

> Save time by using the arrow keys on your calculator to change the power for each new calculation.

........5........ ✓ years
(Total for Question 11 is 3 marks)

*12 The diagram shows Bridget's new sewing box and a knitting needle.

Diagram **NOT**
drawn accurately

> You can add lines to the diagram to show the triangles you are using.

Will the knitting needle fit inside the box?
You must show all of your working.

$BD^2 = BA^2 + AD^2 = 25^2 + 20^2 = 1025$ ✓
$DF^2 = BD^2 + 10^2 = 1025 + 100 = 1125$ ✓
$DF = \sqrt{1125} = 33.5410...$ cm ✓
33 cm is less than 33.5410... cm

> You need to work out the length of the longest diagonal in the box. You could also use the formula for Pythagoras' theorem in 3 dimensions:
> $DF^2 = DA^2 + AB^2 + BF^2$

Yes, the knitting needle will fit. ✓

(Total for Question 12 is 4 marks)

13 The diagram shows three squares.

Diagram **NOT**
drawn accurately

A (x)   B ($x + 1$)   C (3)

The area of square **C** is equal to the total area of squares **A** and **B**.

(a) Show that $x^2 + x = 4$

$x^2 + (x + 1)^2 = 3^2$ ✓
$x^2 + x^2 + 2x + 1 = 9$
$2x^2 + 2x + 1 = 9$
$2x^2 + 2x = 8$
$x^2 + x = 4$ ✓✓

> This question says 'Show that' so the working is the answer. Make sure that you write out every line of your working.

(3)

(b) Use a trial and improvement method to find the value of x.
Give your answer correct to 1 decimal place.
You must show all of your working.

x	$x^2 + x$	Too big or too small?
1	2	Too small
2	6	Too big ✓
1.5	3.75	Too small
1.6	4.16	Too big
1.55	3.9525	Too small ✓✓

> Work out $x^2 + x$ for different values of x and compare the result to 4. Use a table like this to keep track of your working.

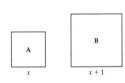

> You need to try $x = 1.55$ to check whether x is closer to 1.5 or 1.6.

$x = $ ....1.6........ ✓
(4)
(Total for Question 13 is 7 marks)

14 The table shows the services provided to the customers of a gas and electricity company.

Service	Gas only	Electricity only	Gas and electricity
Number of customers	70 000	84 000	126 000

The company wants to interview a stratified sample of 200 of its customers.

Work out the number of customers to include in the sample who receive both gas and electricity.

$70\,000 + 84\,000 + 126\,000 = 280\,000$

$126\,000 \times \dfrac{200}{280\,000} = 90$ ✓

> The sampling fraction is:
> $\dfrac{200}{70\,000 + 84\,000 + 126\,000}$

> You could also work out the proportion of the population who receive both gas and electricity, then multiply this by the sample size:
> $\dfrac{126\,000}{280\,000} \times 200 = 90$

........90........ ✓
(Total for Question 14 is 2 marks)

30

31

32

33

133

15 Make a the subject of the formula

$$4b = m(2 - a)$$

$$\frac{4b}{m} = 2 - a \quad \checkmark$$

$$\frac{4b}{m} + a = 2 \quad \checkmark$$

$$a = 2 - \frac{4b}{m}$$

> Use inverse operations to get a on its own on one side of the formula.

$$a = 2 - \frac{4b}{m} \quad \checkmark$$

(Total for Question 15 is 3 marks)

16 The amount of fruit juice bought for a function was 60 litres, to the nearest litre.

(a) Write down the lower bound for the amount of juice bought.

> The smallest number which gives 60 when rounded to the nearest whole number is 59.5.

59.5 $\checkmark$ litres

(1)

The fruit juice was poured into glasses with a capacity of 200 ml, to the nearest 10 ml.

(b) Work out the minimum number of glasses which could be filled.
Give your answer to the nearest whole number.

$$59\,500 \div 205 = 290.2439... \quad \checkmark$$

> You need to consider the worst-case scenario. Divide the lower bound for the amount of fruit juice by the upper bound for the capacity of each glass. Remember to convert the amount of fruit juice from litres to ml by multiplying by 1000.

290 $\checkmark$

(2)

(Total for Question 16 is 3 marks)

---

17 The diagram shows a metal rivet made by joining a hemisphere to a cylinder.

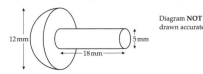

Diagram **NOT** drawn accurately

Work out the volume of metal used to make the rivet.
Give your answer correct to 3 significant figures.

<u>Hemisphere</u>

$$\frac{2}{3} \times \pi \times 6^3 = 144\pi \quad \checkmark$$

> The volume of a sphere is given on the formula sheet. It is $\frac{4}{3}\pi r^3$, so the volume of the hemisphere is $\frac{2}{3}\pi r^3$. Divide the diameter of the hemisphere by 2 to get the radius.

<u>Cylinder</u>

$$\pi \times 2.5^2 \times 18 = \frac{225}{2}\pi \quad \checkmark$$

$$144\pi + \frac{225}{2}\pi = \frac{513}{2}\pi \quad \checkmark$$

$$= 805.8185156...$$

> The volume of a cylinder is $\pi r^2 h$. You should learn this as it is not given on the formula sheet.

> Don't use rounded values in your calculations. Leave answers in terms of π or write down all the digits from your calculator display.

806 $\checkmark$ mm³

(Total for Question 17 is 4 marks)

18

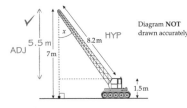

Diagram **NOT** drawn accurately

> $7 - 1.5 = 5.5$
> Write the missing length on the diagram.

The diagram shows a mobile crane.

Calculate the size of angle x correct to 1 decimal place.

$$\cos x = \frac{\text{ADJ}}{\text{HYP}}$$

$$= \frac{5.5}{8.2} \quad \checkmark$$

$$x = \cos^{-1}\left(\frac{5.5}{8.2}\right) \quad \checkmark$$

$$= 47.8764...°$$

> Remember to label the sides of your triangle relative to the angle you are trying to find.

> You can't 'divide by cos' to get x on its own. Use the $\cos^{-1}$ function on your calculator.

47.9 $\checkmark$ °

(Total for Question 18 is 4 marks)

---

*19 The diagram shows a cannon ball being fired horizontally from the top of a cliff.

After t seconds, the height h metres of the ball is given by the equation $h = 75 - 5t^2$

Use a graphical method to estimate how long it takes for the ball to reach a height of 40 metres.

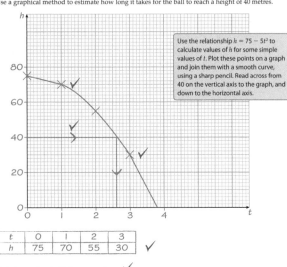

> Use the relationship $h = 75 - 5t^2$ to calculate values of h for some simple values of t. Plot these points on a graph and join them with a smooth curve, using a sharp pencil. Read across from 40 on the vertical axis to the graph, and down to the horizontal axis.

t	0	1	2	3
h	75	70	55	30	$\checkmark$

It takes about 2.6 seconds. $\checkmark$

(Total for Question 19 is 5 marks)

20 The table gives some information about the heights of advertisements in a newspaper.

Height (h cm)	Frequency f	Midpoint x	$f \times x$
$0 < h \leqslant 10$	19	5	95
$10 < h \leqslant 15$	17	12.5	212.5
$15 < h \leqslant 20$	12	17.5	210
$20 < h \leqslant 25$	7	22.5	157.5
$25 < h \leqslant 40$	8	32.5	260
Totals	63		935

✓ ✓

One of the advertisements is chosen at random.

(a) Work out the probability that the height of the advertisement is greater than 15 cm.

$12 + 7 + 8 = 27$

$19 + 17 + 12 + 7 + 8 = 63$ ✓

$\dfrac{27}{63} = \dfrac{3}{7}$

> Work out the number of advertisements whose height was greater than 15 cm and divide this by the total number of advertisements.

> You don't need to cancel fractions in probability questions – you could leave your answer as $\frac{27}{63}$.

$\dfrac{3}{7}$ ✓

(2)

(b) Write down the modal class.

> The class with the largest frequency is the modal class.

$0 < h \leqslant 10$ ✓

(1)

(c) Work out an estimate for the mean height of an advertisement.
Give your answer to 1 decimal place.

Estimate of mean $= \dfrac{\text{sum of } f \times x \text{ column}}{\text{sum of } f \text{ column}}$

$= \dfrac{935}{63}$ ✓

$= 14.8412...$

> Add columns to the table for 'Midpoint' and 'Frequency × Midpoint'.

14.8 ✓ cm

(4)

(Question 20 continued on next page)

(d) On the grid, draw a histogram for the information in the table.

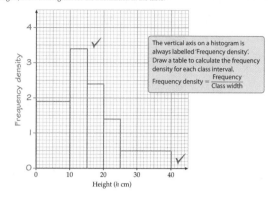

> The vertical axis on a histogram is always labelled 'Frequency density'. Draw a table to calculate the frequency density for each class interval.
> Frequency density $= \dfrac{\text{Frequency}}{\text{Class width}}$

Height (h cm)	Frequency	Class width	Frequency density
$0 < h \leqslant 10$	19	10	$19 \div 10 = 1.9$
$10 < h \leqslant 15$	17	5	$17 \div 5 = 3.4$
$15 < h \leqslant 20$	12	5	$12 \div 5 = 2.4$
$20 < h \leqslant 25$	7	5	$7 \div 5 = 1.4$
$25 < h \leqslant 40$	8	15	$8 \div 15 = 0.5$ (1 d.p.)

✓

(3)

(Total for Question 20 is 10 marks)

21

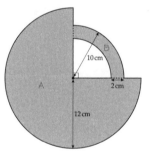

Diagram **NOT** drawn accurately

The shape is made using parts of circles.

Work out the shaded area.
Give your answer correct to 3 significant figures.

Section A

$\dfrac{3}{4} \times \pi \times 12^2 = 108\pi$ ✓

> Section A is $\frac{3}{4}$ of a circle of radius 12 cm.
> Section B is $\frac{1}{4}$ of a circle of radius 10 cm minus $\frac{1}{4}$ of a circle of radius 8 cm.

Section B

$\dfrac{1}{4} \times \pi \times 10^2 - \dfrac{1}{4} \times \pi \times 8^2 = 9\pi$ ✓

$108\pi + 9\pi = 117\pi$ ✓

$= 367.5663405...$

> The area of a circle is πr^2. Remember this, as it is not given on the formula sheet.

> Don't use rounded values in your calculations. Leave answers in terms of π or write down all the digits from your calculator display.

368 cm² ✓

(Total for Question 21 is 4 marks)

22 The graph of $y = f(x)$ is shown on the grid below.
The coordinates of the minimum point on the curve are $(2, -4)$.

> The transformation $f(x) \rightarrow f(ax)$ is a stretch in the horizontal direction, with scale factor $\frac{1}{a}$. So the graph of $f\left(\frac{1}{2}x\right)$ is stretched in the horizontal direction with a scale factor of 2. Each point on the new graph is twice as far away from the y-axis.

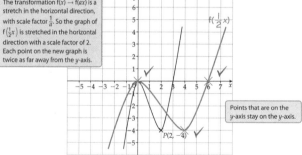

> Points that are on the y-axis stay on the y-axis.

(a) Write down the coordinates of the minimum point of the curve with equation $f\left(\frac{1}{2}x\right)$.

$(4, -4)$ ✓

(1)

(b) On the grid, sketch the graph of $f\left(\frac{1}{2}x\right)$.

> Work out where all the key points should be and then join them with a smooth curve.

(3)

(Total for Question 22 is 4 marks)

23 Write $\dfrac{3x-1}{2} - \dfrac{2x+1}{3}$ as a single fraction in its simplest form.

$\dfrac{3x-1}{2} - \dfrac{2x+1}{3} = \dfrac{3(3x-1)}{6} - \dfrac{2(2x+1)}{6}$ ✓

$= \dfrac{3(3x-1) - 2(2x+1)}{6}$ ✓

$= \dfrac{9x - 3 - 4x - 2}{6}$

$= \dfrac{5x - 5}{6}$

> Multiply the numerator and denominator of the first fraction by 3, and multiply the numerator and denominator of the second fraction by 2.

> Once the fractions have the same denominator you can subtract the numerators.

> $5x - 5$ and 6 have no common factors, so this fraction is in simplest form.

> You could also write $\dfrac{5(x-1)}{6}$

$\dfrac{5x - 5}{6}$ ✓

(Total for Question 23 is 3 marks)

24 Solve $2x^2 - 8x - 3 = 0$
Give your solutions correct to 3 significant figures.

$a = 2,\ b = -8,\ c = -3$

$x = \dfrac{-(-8) \pm \sqrt{(-8)^2 - 4 \times 2 \times (-3)}}{2 \times 2}$ ✓

$= \dfrac{8 \pm \sqrt{64 + 24}}{4}$

$= \dfrac{8 \pm \sqrt{88}}{4}$ ✓

$= \dfrac{8 + 9.3808...}{4}$ or $\dfrac{8 - 9.3808...}{4}$

$= 4.3452...$ or $-0.3452...$

> The quadratic formula is given on the formula sheet. You can use it to solve quadratic equations on your calculator paper:
> $x = \dfrac{-b \pm \sqrt{b^2 - 4ac}}{2a}$
> Write down the values of a, b and c before you substitute.

$x = 4.35$ or $x = -0.345$ ✓

(Total for Question 24 is 3 marks)

25

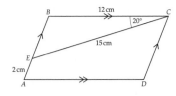

Diagram **NOT** drawn accurately

ABCD is a parallelogram.

$BC = 12$ cm.
$EC = 15$ cm.
$AE = 2$ cm.
Angle $ECB = 20°$.

Calculate the area of the parallelogram.
Give your answer correct to 1 decimal place.
Show all of your working.

$EB^2 = 12^2 + 15^2 - 2 \times 12 \times 15 \times \cos 20°$ ✓

$EB^2 = 30.7106...$ ✓

$EB = 5.5417...$

$\dfrac{\sin B}{15} = \dfrac{\sin 20°}{5.5417...}$ ✓

$\sin B = \dfrac{15 \times \sin 20°}{5.5417...}$

$= 0.9257...$

$AB = 2 + 5.5417...$

$= 7.5417...$

> Plan your answer and show all your working. To work out the area you need to:
> • calculate EB using the cosine rule
> • calculate $\angle EBC$ using the sine rule
> • use $\angle EBC$ and the sides AB and BC to calculate the area of the parallelogram.

> The area of the shaded triangle is $\frac{1}{2} \times AB \times BC \times \sin B$
>
> The area of the whole parallelogram is twice the area of the triangle.

✓

Area $ABCD = 2 \times \dfrac{1}{2} \times 7.5417... \times 12 \times \sin B = 83.7818...$

> These formulae are on the formula sheet.
> In any triangle *ABC*:
> Area of triangle $= \frac{1}{2} ab \sin C$
> Sine rule: $\dfrac{a}{\sin A} = \dfrac{b}{\sin B} = \dfrac{c}{\sin C}$
> Cosine rule: $a^2 = b^2 + c^2 - 2bc \cos A$
>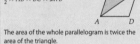

83.8 ✓ .... cm²

(Total for Question 25 is 5 marks)

TOTAL FOR PAPER IS 100 MARKS

1 Fernando gets £20 as a birthday present.

He spends £5 on a magazine.

(a) Express £5 as a fraction of £20
Write your answer in its simplest form.

$$\frac{5}{20} = \frac{1}{4}$$

$\frac{1}{4}$ ✓

(1)

Fernando puts £3 into his savings.

(b) Express £3 as a percentage of £20

> Write $\frac{3}{20}$ as an equivalent fraction with denominator 100.
> You could also write $\frac{3}{20}$ as a decimal, then multiply by 100.

$$\frac{3}{20} = \frac{15}{100} = 15\%$$

15 ✓ %
✓

(2)

Fernando spends the remaining £12 on a pack of cards and some sweets.
The cards cost £2.50 more than the sweets.

(c) How much did he spend on the sweets?

$$x + (x + 2.5) = 12 \quad ✓$$
$$2x + 2.5 = 12$$
$$2x = 9.5$$
$$x = 4.75$$

> If the sweets cost £x, then the cards cost £$(x + 2.5)$. Use this information to write an equation and solve it to find x.

£ 4.75 ✓

(2)

(Total for Question 1 is 5 marks)

*2

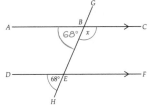

Diagram **NOT**
drawn accurately

ABC and DEF are parallel lines.
$GBEH$ is a straight line.
Angle $DEH = 68°$.

Work out the size of the angle marked x.
Give reasons for your answer.

$\angle ABE = 68°$
Corresponding angles on parallel lines are equal.

$$180 - 68 = 112 \quad ✓$$
$$x = 112° \quad ✓$$

Angles on a straight line add up to 180°. ✓

> Label any angles you work out on the diagram. But make sure you still give a reason for each step of your working.

(Total for Question 2 is 3 marks)

*3 A fair three-sided spinner has sections labelled 1, 2 and 4
A fair four-sided dice has faces labelled 1, 2, 3 and 4

The spinner is spun and the dice is rolled at the same time.
The number the spinner lands on is added to the number shown on the dice to give a total score.

Work out the probability that the total score is less than 5

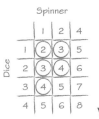

> Draw a sample space diagram to show all the possible outcomes. There are 12 outcomes in total. 5 outcomes have a total score less than 5, so the probability of a total score less than 5 is $\frac{5}{12}$.

$\frac{5}{12}$ ✓

(Total for Question 3 is 3 marks)

4 Femke asked 100 adults where they spent their summer holiday.
Each adult either spent their holiday in the UK or they spent their holiday abroad.

Of the 36 people who spent their holiday in the UK, 26 were men.
35 women asked spent their holiday abroad.

How many more men spent their holiday abroad than in the UK?

	UK	Abroad	Total
M	26	29	55
F	10	35	45
Total	36	64	100	✓✓

> You can use a two-way table to answer this question. Fill in the information given in the question, then use addition and subtraction to work out and fill in the missing values.

$$29 - 26 = 3$$
✓

3 ✓

(Total for Question 4 is 4 marks)

5 Eve is the manager at a supermarket.
She thinks that more tills must be opened because customers have to wait too long before being served.
To see if this is true she records the time, in minutes, that 19 customers have to wait before being served.

The table shows her results.

28	14	21	15	25	40	47	22	38	35
62	46	30	23	36	42	26	18	15	

(a) Draw an ordered stem and leaf diagram for this data.

```
0 | 5
1 | 5 8
2 | 1 2 5 6
3 | 0 3 5 6 8 8
4 | 0 2 4 6 7
5 |
6 | 2          ✓✓
```

Key: 1 | 5 = 1.5 minutes ✓

> Cross off each data value as you add it to your stem and leaf diagram. Remember to add a key, and check that you have 19 'leaves' and that they are in order of size.

(3)

Eve opens more tills at the supermarket if the median waiting time is more than 3 minutes.

(b) Does Eve open more tills?
You must explain your answer.

> There are 19 data values so the median is the $\frac{19+1}{2}$th value. Compare this time with 3 minutes and write a conclusion.

Median = $\frac{19+1}{2}$ = 10th value ✓

Median = 3.5 minutes ✓

3.5 minutes is more than 3 minutes, so Eve does open more tills. ✓

(3)
(Total for Question 5 is 6 marks)

48

---

*6 Emir works 120 hours per month.
He is paid £8 per hour.

His rent is £400 per month.

Emir gets a pay rise of 5%.

His rent increases to £430 per month.

Is Emir better off or worse off each month?
You must show your working.

Before
120 × 8 = 960
960 − 400 = 560 ✓
✓

> 12 × 8 = 96, so 120 × 8 = 960

> Work out how much money Emir has after he pays his rent. Compare the amounts before and after his pay rise and write a conclusion.

After
10% of 960 = 96
5% of 960 = 48
960 + 48 = 1008

> To find 5% of £960 find 10% then divide it by 2. You need to increase £960 by 5% so add £48 on to £960.

$\overset{9}{\cancel{10}}08$
− 430 ✓
 578 ✓

> You could also work out Emir's extra monthly pay and compare that with his £30 rent increase.

£578 is more than £560 so he is better off after the pay rise. ✓

(Total for Question 6 is 5 marks)

49

---

*7

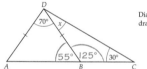

Diagram NOT drawn accurately

ABC is a straight line.
BD = AD.
Angle BCD = 30°.
Angle ADB = 70°.

Work out the size of the angle marked x.
Give reasons for your answer.

$\frac{180 - 70}{2} = \frac{110}{2} = 55$ ✓

∠ABD = 55°

Base angles in an isosceles triangle are equal. ✓

180 − 55 = 125

∠DBC = 125° ✓

Angles on a straight line add up to 180°.

180 − 125 − 30 = 25

x = 25° ✓

Angles in a triangle add up to 180°.

> Write any angles you work out on your diagram, and remember to give reasons for each step of your working.

(Total for Question 7 is 4 marks)

50

---

8 Solve the equation

$$3x + 2 = 7x - 8$$

> You could subtract 7x from both sides, but it's easier if you keep the x term positive. Remember: solutions to equations can be positive or negative numbers, or fractions.

2 = 4x − 8
10 = 4x ✓
$\frac{10}{4}$ = x
2.5 = x

> Follow these steps:
> • subtract 3x from both sides
> • add 8 to both sides
> • divide both sides by 4.

x = 2.5 ✓
(Total for Question 8 is 2 marks)

9 The diagram shows a solid prism made from plastic.
The cross section of the prism is a right-angled triangle.

Diagram NOT drawn accurately

The density of the plastic is 0.5 g/cm³.

Calculate the mass of the prism.

$\frac{1}{2}$ × 3 × 4 = 6 ✓

6 × 5 = 30 ✓

> Use these formulae:
> • Area of a triangle = $\frac{1}{2}$ × base × height
> • Volume of a prism = area of cross-section × length
> • Mass = Density × Volume
> You can draw the formula triangle for density to help you remember the last formula.

M = D × V
  = 0.5 × 30 ✓
  = 15

15 ✓ grams
(Total for Question 9 is 3 marks)

51

138

10 In a restaurant, tables can be placed together for large numbers of people.

The diagram shows chairs arranged around tables.

Find an expression, in terms of n, for the number of chairs at n tables.

Number of tables (n)	1	2	3	4	5
Number of chairs	4	6	8	10	12

+2 +2 +2 +2

> The term-to-term rule is 'add 2'. So the nth term will be $2n \pm \square$. Compare $2n$ with each term to work out what you need to add or subtract.

$2n + 2$ ✓ ✓

....

(Total for Question 10 is 2 marks)

11 (a) Simplify $y^6 \div y^3$

> $a^m \div a^n = a^{m-n}$

y^3 ✓

(1)

(b) Simplify $3x^3 \times 4x^5$

$3 \times 4 \times x^3 \times x^5$ ✓

> $a^m \times a^n = a^{m+n}$

$12x^8$ ✓

(2)

(c) Write down the value of 12^0

> $a^0 = 1$

1 ✓

(1)

(d) Work out the value of $8^{\frac{2}{3}}$

$(\sqrt[3]{8})^2 = 2^2 = 4$

> $(a^m)^n = a^{m \times n}$ and $a^{\frac{1}{n}} = \sqrt[n]{a}$

4 ✓

✓

(2)

$3^x = \frac{1}{9}$

(e) Write down the value of x.

$\frac{1}{9} = \frac{1}{3^2} = 3^{-2}$

> $a^{-n} = \frac{1}{a^n}$

$x = -2$ ✓

(1)

(Total for Question 11 is 7 marks)

12

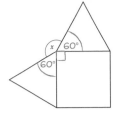

Diagram **NOT** drawn accurately

The diagram shows a square and two equilateral triangles.

Sham says 'I could fit three more equilateral triangles around the corner of the square marked with the x.'

Explain why Sham is wrong.

$360 - 90 - 60 - 60 = 150°$ ✓

$3 \times 60 = 180°$ ✓

> Work out the size of angle x, and work out how much space would be needed for 3 equilateral triangles. Remember that all the angles in an equilateral triangle are 60°. Make sure you write a conclusion in words.

x is only 150° and Sham would need 180° for 3 equilateral triangles. ✓

....

....

....

(Total for Question 12 is 3 marks)

13 The diagram shows the graph of $y = x^2 + 3x - 2$

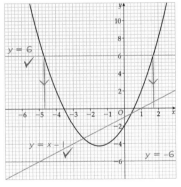

> For part (a) (ii) draw the line $y = 6$ on your graph with a ruler and a sharp pencil. Draw lines to show the values you are reading off.

> For part (c) draw the line $y = x - 1$ on the graph.

(a) Use the graph to find estimates for the solutions of

(i) $x^2 + 3x - 2 = 0$

$x = 0.6$ and $x = -3.6$ ✓

> The solutions are the x-coordinates at the points where the curve crosses the x-axis.

(1)

(ii) $x^2 + 3x - 2 = 6$

$x = 1.7$ and $x = -4.7$ ✓

> The solutions are the x-coordinates at the points where the graph intersects with the line $y = 6$.

(2)

(b) Can you use the graph to find estimates for the solutions of $x^2 + 3x - 2 = -6$? Explain your answer.

No. The graph does not intersect with the line $y = -6$. ✓

....

(1)

(c) Use the graph to find estimates for the solutions of the simultaneous equations

$y = x^2 + 3x - 2$
$y = x - 1$

> The solutions are the coordinates at the points where the graph intersects with the line $y = x - 1$. Remember each solution is an x-coordinate and a y-coordinate.

$x = 0.4, y = -0.6$ ✓ or

$x = -2.4, y = -3.4$ ✓

(3)

(Total for Question 13 is 7 marks)

14 (a) Work out the value of $(5 \times 10^4) \times (5 \times 10^5)$
Give your answer in standard form.

$5 \times 5 \times 10^4 \times 10^5 = 25 \times 10^9$ ✓

$= 2.5 \times 10^{10}$

> 25×10^9 is not in standard form, because 25 is larger than 10.
> $25 \times 10^9 = 2.5 \times 10 \times 10^9 = 2.5 \times 10^{10}$

2.5×10^{10} ✓

(2)

(b) Work out the value of $(5 \times 10^4) + (5 \times 10^5)$
Give your answer in standard form.

50000
$+500000$
$\overline{550000}$ ✓

> To add numbers in standard form write them out in full. Remember to convert your answer back into standard form.

5.5×10^5 ✓

(2)

(Total for Question 14 is 4 marks)

15 A music download website sells singles and albums.

The music download website makes 1000 sales in one hour. The income for this hour is £1500.

Singles cost 50p to download. Albums cost £4.50 to download.

How many singles does the website sell in this hour?

> Use the information given in the question to set up two simultaneous equations. Make sure you write the costs of both types of download in the same units.

① $S + A = 1000$
② $0.5S + 4.5A = 1500$ ✓

$2 \times ②$ $S + 9A = 3000$ ✓
$- ①$ $S + A = 1000$
$8A = 2000$ ✓
$A = 250$

> Use S to represent the number of singles downloaded and A to represent the number of albums downloaded.
> • Total downloads = 1000, so $S + A = 1000$
> • Total income = £1500, so $0.5S + 4.5A = 1500$

$S + A = 1000$
$S + 250 = 1000$
$S = 750$

> You can use the other equation to check your answer:
> $0.5S + 4.5A = 0.5 \times 750 + 4.5 \times 250$
> $= 375 + 1125$
> $= 1500$ ✓

750 ✓

(Total for Question 15 is 4 marks)

16 The diagram shows a triangle.

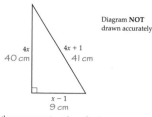

Diagram **NOT** drawn accurately

In the diagram, all the measurements are in centimetres.

The perimeter of the triangle is 90 cm.
The area of the triangle is A cm².

Work out the value of A.

$4x + (x - 1) + (4x + 1) = 90$ ✓

$9x = 90$

$x = 10$ ✓

$A = \frac{1}{2} \times 9 \times 40 = 9 \times 20 = 180$ ✓

Follow these steps:
- form an equation
- solve your equation to find the value of x
- write the actual lengths on the diagram
- work out the area of the triangle.

$A = \underline{\quad 180 \quad}$ ✓ cm²

(Total for Question 16 is 4 marks)

***17**

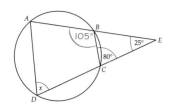

Diagram **NOT** drawn accurately

A, B, C and D are four points on the circumference of a circle.

AB and DC are extended to meet at E.

Angle $BCE = 80°$.
Angle $BEC = 25°$.

Work out the size of angle x.
You must give reasons for your working.

$80 + 25 = 105$

$\angle ABC = 105°$ ✓

Exterior angle of a triangle is equal to the sum of the two opposite interior angles.

$180 - 105 = 75$

$x = 75°$ ✓

Opposite angles in a cyclic quadrilateral add up to $180°$. ✓

AD and BC are not parallel, so $\angle ADC$ and $\angle BCE$ are not corresponding angles.

Write any angles you work out on your diagram.

This is a useful reason when solving angle problems:

$a = b + c$

(Total for Question 17 is 3 marks)

---

18 The cumulative frequency graph shows the amounts of time spent by students using a mobile phone to access the internet in one day.

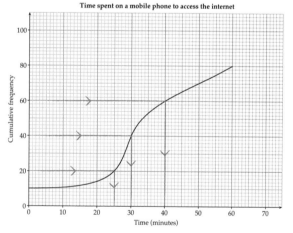

Use the graph to estimate

(a) how many students did not use a mobile phone to access the internet

$\underline{\quad 10 \quad}$ ✓ students

(1)

(b) the median

There are 80 data values. Read across from 40 and down to the horizontal axis.

$\underline{\quad 30 \quad}$ ✓ minutes

(1)

(c) the interquartile range.

$40 - 25 = 15$ ✓

Read across from 20 to estimate the lower quartile and from 60 to estimate the upper quartile.

Interquartile range = upper quartile − lower quartile

$\underline{\quad 15 \quad}$ ✓ minutes

(2)

(Total for Question 18 is 4 marks)

---

19 y is inversely proportional to the square of x.
When $x = 10$, $y = 1$

(a) Write an equation for y in terms of x.

$y = \frac{k}{x^2}$ ✓

$1 = \frac{k}{10^2}$ ✓

$1 = \frac{k}{100}$

$100 = k$

Write a formila connecting y and x. Use the values given in the equation to work out the proportionality constant, k.

$y = \underline{\quad \frac{100}{x^2} \quad}$ ✓

(3)

(b) Work out a value of x when $y = 400$

$y = \frac{100}{x^2}$

$400 = \frac{100}{x^2}$ ✓

$400x^2 = 100$

$x^2 = \frac{1}{4}$

$x = \pm \sqrt{\frac{1}{4}}$

$= \pm \frac{1}{2}$

Substitute $y = 400$ into your formula. You need to solve an equation to find the value of x.

The question asks for **a value** so you could write $\frac{1}{2}$ or $-\frac{1}{2}$.

$x = \underline{\quad \frac{1}{2} \quad}$ ✓

(2)

(Total for Question 19 is 5 marks)

20 The diagram shows a quadrilateral $ABCD$.

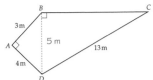

Diagram **NOT** drawn accurately

$AB = 3$ m.
$AD = 4$ m.
$CD = 13$ m.
Angle BAD = angle $CBD = 90°$.

Calculate the length of BC.
You must show your working.

> You need to use Pythagoras' theorem twice – once on triangle ABD and once on triangle BCD. Show all your working, and write any lengths you work out on the diagram.

$$BD^2 = 3^2 + 4^2 = 9 + 16$$
$$= 25 \checkmark$$
$$BD = \sqrt{25}$$
$$= 5 \checkmark$$

$$BC^2 = 13^2 - 5^2 = 169 - 25$$
$$= 144 \checkmark$$
$$BC = \sqrt{144}$$
$$= 12 \checkmark$$

.... 12 $\checkmark$ m
(Total for Question 20 is 5 marks)

---

21 Bag A contains six 10p coins and two 2p coins.
Bag B contains five 10p coins and three 2p coins.

A coin is taken at random from Bag A and placed in Bag B.
A coin is then taken at random from Bag B and placed in Bag A.

Calculate the probability that Bag B finishes with exactly 64p.

$$5 \times 10 + 3 \times 2 = 56$$
$$56 + 10 - 2 = 64 \checkmark$$

> Bag B contains 56p at the start. If you add 10p then remove 2p you will be left with 64p.

First pick (A $\longrightarrow$ B)
$$P(10) = \frac{6}{8}$$

Second pick (B $\longrightarrow$ A)
$$P(2) = \frac{3}{9} \checkmark$$

> For the second pick, there are now 9 coins in bag B. Three of them are 2p coins, so the probability is $\frac{3}{9}$.

$$\frac{6}{8} \times \frac{3}{9} = \frac{18}{72}$$

> You could cancel this fraction to $\frac{1}{4}$, but you don't need to cancel fractions in probability questions.

.... $\frac{18}{72}$ $\checkmark$
(Total for Question 21 is 3 marks)

---

22 Expand and simplify $(\sqrt{27} + \sqrt{3})^2$

$$(\sqrt{27} + \sqrt{3})(\sqrt{27} + \sqrt{3}) = (\sqrt{27})^2 + \sqrt{27}\sqrt{3} + \sqrt{27}\sqrt{3} + (\sqrt{3})^2 \checkmark$$
$$= 27 + \sqrt{81} + \sqrt{81} + 3 \checkmark \quad \boxed{\sqrt{a}\sqrt{b} = \sqrt{ab}}$$
$$= 27 + 9 + 9 + 3$$
$$= 48$$

.... 48 $\checkmark$
(Total for Question 22 is 3 marks)

---

23 Three vases are mathematically similar in shape.

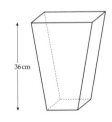

Volume = 800 cm³   Surface area = 400 cm²

The smallest vase has a height of 12 cm and a volume of 800 cm³.
The medium vase has a height of 24 cm and a surface area of 400 cm².
The largest vase has a height of 36 cm.

(a) Work out the surface area of the smallest vase.

$$24 \div 12 = 2$$
$$2^2 = 4$$
$$400 \div 4 = 100$$
$$\checkmark$$

> The scale factor for length is 2 so the scale factor for surface area is $2^2 = 4$.

.... 100 $\checkmark$ cm²
(2)

(b) Work out the volume of the largest vase.

$$36 \div 12 = 3$$
$$3^3 = 27$$
$$800 \times 27 = 21600$$
$$\checkmark$$

> The scale factor for length is 3 so the scale factor for volume is $3^3 = 27$.

$800 \times 20 = 16000$	
$800 \times 7 = 5600$	
$800 \times 27 = 21600$	

.... 21 600 $\checkmark$ cm³
(2)
(Total for Question 23 is 4 marks)

---

24 The two diagrams both show the function $y = f(x)$
Point P is a point on the function at coordinates $(5, 1)$.

Graph A   Graph B

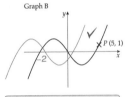
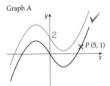

> $f(x) \rightarrow f(x) + a$ is a transformation $\binom{0}{a}$

> $f(x) \rightarrow f(x + a)$ is a transformation $\binom{-a}{0}$

(a) (i) On graph A sketch the function $y = f(x) + 2$
   (ii) Write down the coordinates of point P after the transformation $y = f(x) + 2$

   (.........5........, ...3.......) $\checkmark$
   (2)

(b) (i) On graph B sketch the function $y = f(x + 2)$
   (ii) Write down the coordinates of point P after the transformation $y = f(x + 2)$

   (.........3........, ...1.......) $\checkmark$
   (2)
   (Total for Question 24 is 4 marks)

---

*25 The nth term for the sequence of triangular numbers is

$$\frac{1}{2}n(n + 1)$$

Prove that the sum of two consecutive triangular numbers is a square number.

> The question says 'Prove' so you need to write down every step of your working clearly.

$$\frac{1}{2}n(n + 1) + \frac{1}{2}(n + 1)((n + 1) + 1) = \frac{1}{2}n(n + 1) + \frac{1}{2}(n + 1)(n + 2)$$

> If $\frac{1}{2}n(n + 1)$ is a triangular number, then $\frac{1}{2}(n + 1)((n + 1) + 1)$ is the next triangular number. Add these expressions together and simplify as much as possible. You can write the expression as $(n + 1)^2$ so it must be a square number.

$$= \frac{1}{2}(n + 1)(n + (n + 2))$$
$$= \frac{1}{2}(n + 1)(2n + 2) \checkmark$$
$$= \frac{1}{2}(n + 1) \times 2(n + 1)$$
$$= (n + 1)(n + 1)$$
$$= (n + 1)^2 \checkmark$$

(Total for Question 25 is 3 marks)

TOTAL FOR PAPER IS 100 MARKS

1 A biased spinner has the numbers 1, 2, 3 and 4

The table shows the probability of some of the numbers on the spinner.

Number	1	2	3	4
Probability	0.3	0.4		

The probability of the spinner landing on 3 is the same as the probability of the spinner landing on 4

(a) Work out the probability that the spinner lands on 4

$1 - 0.3 - 0.4 = 0.3$

$0.3 \div 2 = 0.15$ ✓

> The probabilities of all the mutually exclusive outcomes of an event add up to 1.

.......................0.15 ✓
(2)

The spinner is spun 120 times.

(b) Work out the likely number of times the spinner lands on 2

$0.4 \times 120 = 48$ ✓

> Expected number of 2s = P(2) × Number of spins

.......................48 ✓
(2)
(Total for Question 1 is 4 marks)

2 Use your calculator to work out

$$\frac{\sqrt{48.3}}{3.75 \times 11.1}$$

Write down all the figures on your calculator display.

$6.949820142... \div 41.625 = 0.166962646...$ ✓

> Write down what the top of the fraction and the bottom of the fraction come to. You can check by entering the calculation in one go on your calculator using the fraction key.

.......................0.166962646... ✓
(Total for Question 2 is 2 marks)

*3 A supermarket sells strawberries in boxes of two different sizes.

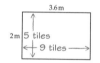
400 g £1.25   900 g £2.95

Which is the better value for money?
You must show your working.

400 g
$400 \div 1.25 = 320$ g/£ ✓

900 g
$900 \div 2.95 = 305.0847...$ g/£ ✓

The 400 g box is better value. ✓

> Divide the weight of each box by the cost in pounds to work out how many grams of strawberries you get per pound (£) in each box. You get more strawberries per £ in the 400 g box, so it is better value for money.

(Total for Question 3 is 3 marks)

*4 Harry works in a paint shop.
He is going to make some green paint.

He needs to mix white paint, blue paint and yellow paint in the ratio 1 : 4 : 5 by volume.

Harry wants to make 300 litres of green paint.

Harry has
25 litres of white paint
125 litres of blue paint
225 litres of yellow paint.

Does Harry have enough white paint, blue paint and yellow paint to make the green paint?

$1 + 4 + 5 = 10$

$300 \div 10 = 30$ ✓

> Divide 300 in the ratio 1 : 4 : 5.
> There are 10 parts in the ratio in total so each part is worth 300 ÷ 10 = 30 litres.

White
$1 \times 30 = 30$ litres ✓
Not enough

Blue
$4 \times 30 = 120$ litres ✓
Enough

> You need to work out all three colours and say whether Harry has enough of each.

Yellow
$5 \times 30 = 150$ litres ✓
Enough

(Total for Question 4 is 4 marks)

5 The diagram shows a line segment, *AB*.

Using compasses and a straight edge, construct an angle of 30° at *A*.
You must show all construction lines.

> Construct an angle of 60° and then bisect that angle. Remember to use a sharp pencil and stiff compasses for your constructions, and never rub out any of your construction lines. Remember to label your 30° angle when you have finished.

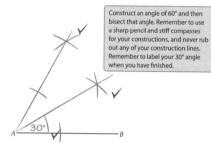

(Total for Question 5 is 3 marks)

6 The formula below can be used to work out the power produced by a wind turbine.

$$P = \frac{D^2 \times W^3}{60}$$

where
P is the power produced in watts
D is the diameter of the wind turbine in metres
W is the wind speed in mph.

The world's largest wind turbine is the Siemens SWT6
It has a diameter of 150 m.

Use the formula to work out the amount of power produced by the Siemens SWT6 when the wind speed is 15 mph.
Give your answer to the nearest 1000 watts.

$\frac{150^2 \times 15^3}{60} = 1\,265\,625$ ✓ ✓

> Write down the exact value from your calculator display before rounding your answer to the nearest 1000.

.......................1 266 000 ✓ watts
(Total for Question 6 is 3 marks)

*7 The diagram shows a porch in the shape of a rectangle.

3.6 m
2 m 5 tiles
9 tiles
Diagram **NOT** drawn accurately

The porch is 3.6 m long and 2 m wide.

Dennis is going to cover the floor of the porch with square floor tiles.

Each floor tile is a square of side 40 cm.
Dennis buys 48 of the floor tiles.

Does Dennis buy enough floor tiles to cover the floor of the porch?
You must show all your working.

$360 \div 40 = 9$ ✓

$200 \div 40 = 5$ ✓

$5 \times 9 = 45$ ✓

Yes ✓

> Convert all the lengths into the same units. Multiply metres by 100 to convert into cm.

> Work out how many tiles you can fit across the porch and how many you can fit up. Dennis needs 5 × 9 = 45 tiles in total and he has 48, so he does have enough.

(Total for Question 7 is 3 marks)

8 Carol is collecting data on photograph downloads.
She chooses a sample of photographs and times how long they take to download.

The frequency table shows the download times for her sample.

Download time, d (seconds)	Frequency
$0 < d \leqslant 10$	2
$10 < d \leqslant 20$	5
$20 < d \leqslant 30$	12
$30 < d \leqslant 40$	22
$40 < d \leqslant 50$	19

(a) How many downloads did Carol complete for her survey?

$2 + 5 + 12 + 22 + 19 = 60$

........60....... ✓
(1)

(b) What is the modal class interval for Carol's data?

> The modal class interval is the class interval with the highest frequency.

........$30 < d \leqslant 40$....... ✓
(1)

(c) Which class interval contains the median?

> $\frac{60 + 1}{2} = 30.5$, so the median is half way between the 30th and 31st values. Both of these values are in the class interval $30 < d \leqslant 40$, so this class interval contains the median.

........$30 < d \leqslant 40$....... ✓
(1)

(d) Explain why it is not possible to calculate the exact mean of this data.

........We don't know the exact data values because data is grouped.... ✓

(1)
(Total for Question 8 is 4 marks)

---

9 Tony goes on holiday to Greece.

He changes £500 into euros (€) to take on holiday.
The exchange rate is £1 = €1.18

On holiday he spends €406

He changes the remaining euros back to pounds when he comes home.
The exchange rate is now £1 = €1.15

How much money does he get back?

$500 \times 1.18 = 590$ ✓
$590 - 406 = 184$ ✓
$184 \div 1.15 = 160$
✓

> Follow these steps:
> - convert £500 into € by multiplying by 1.18
> - subtract €406 from the answer
> - convert the remaining € back into £ at the new exchange rate by dividing by 1.15.

£........160...... ✓
(Total for Question 9 is 4 marks)

---

10 (a) Work out the size of the angle marked x.

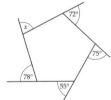

Diagram **NOT** drawn accurately

$78 + 72 + 75 + 55 = 280$
$360 - 280 = 80$

> The exterior angles of any polygon add up to 360°.

✓

........80..... ✓ °
(2)

(b) Work out the size of the interior angle of a regular polygon with 8 sides.

$360 \div 8 = 45$
$180 - 45 = 135$

> Work out the size of one exterior angle. Then subtract this from 180° to work out the size of one interior angle.

✓

> The sum of the interior angles of an 8-sided polygon is $180° \times (8 - 2) = 1080°$. You could also use this fact to work out the size of one angle: $1080° \div 8 = 135°$

........135..... ✓ °
(2)
(Total for Question 10 is 4 marks)

---

*11 Miss Jebson makes an artwork for the wall of her school hall.

The artwork is made from a square panel of wood.
She cuts one rectangular hole and two circular holes out of the square panel of wood.

Each circle has a diameter of 30 cm.
The rectangle is 90 cm long and 20 cm wide.

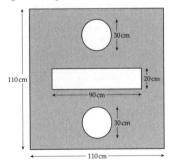

Diagram **NOT** drawn accurately

Miss Jebson is going to paint the front of the artwork with one coat of paint.
One pot of paint covers 2500 cm².

How many pots of paint does Miss Jebson need?
You must show your working.

<u>Square</u>
$110 \times 110 = 12\,100$

> Plan your answer, and write down all your working neatly.

<u>Rectangle</u>
$90 \times 20 = 1800$ ✓

<u>Circle</u>
$\pi \times 15^2 = 225\pi$ ✓

> You can leave answers in terms of π until the end of the calculation.

$12\,100 - 1800 - 2 \times 225\pi = 8886.2833...$ ✓
$8886.2833... \div 2500 = 3.5545...$ ✓
4 pots ✓

> Miss Jebson must buy a whole number of pots, so she needs 4.

(Total for Question 11 is 5 marks)

12 Sam wanted to find out which holiday destinations are popular with families.
He interviewed people at Luton airport in January.

(a) His sample is biased.
Give two reasons to show his sample is biased.

> You could also say that fewer families are likely to go on holiday in January.

1 He only interviewed people at an airport so he didn't interview people who don't fly. ✓

2 Some destinations (like ski resorts) may be more popular in January. ✓

(2)

(b) Write a suitable question Sam could use to find out which holiday destinations are popular with families.

Which country do you like to go on holiday with your family? ✓

☐ UK
☐ France
☐ Spain
☐ Italy
☐ USA
☐ Other ✓

> Keep your question simple.

> Write at least 4 response boxes and make sure you include a box for 'other' so everyone can tick a box.

(2)

(Total for Question 12 is 4 marks)

72

---

13 Alex walks from point A to point P on a bearing of 070°.

Diagram **NOT** drawn accurately

On what bearing must Alex walk to go directly back to point A?

70 + 180 = 250
✓

> Add or subtract 180° to calculate a reverse bearing.

250 ✓ °

(Total for Question 13 is 2 marks)

73

---

14 A perfume house is making two new fragrances.
Each bottle contains 350 m*l*.

'Sparkle' contains cedarwood and lavender in the ratio 2 : 5
'Shimmer' contains cedarwood and lavender in the ratio 5 : 12

Which fragrance, Sparkle or Shimmer, has the greater amount of cedarwood?
You must show your working.

Sparkle
2 + 5 = 7
350 ÷ 7 = 50
2 × 50 = 100 ✓

> Work out the amount of cedarwood in each bottle. For Sparkle there are 2 + 5 = 7 parts in the ratio. So each part is worth 350 ÷ 7 = 50 ml. Multiply this by 2 to work out the amount of cedarwood.

Shimmer
5 + 12 = 17
350 ÷ 17 = 20.5882...
5 × 20.5882 = 102.9411... ✓

> You could also write the amount of cedarwood in each bottle as a fraction, and compare the fractions.

Shimmer ✓

(Total for Question 14 is 3 marks)

15 In an experiment a spring is stretched by 27% to 32.4 cm.

Work out the original length of the spring.
Give your answer correct to 3 significant figures.

100 + 27 = 127
$\frac{127}{100}$ = 1.27 ✓

32.4 ÷ 1.27 = 25.5118...
✓

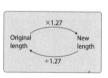

> Write down at least 4 decimal places from your calculator display before you round your answer.

25.5 ✓ cm

(Total for Question 15 is 3 marks)

74

---

16 The diagram shows a solid metal square-based cuboid.

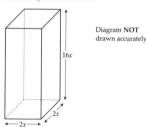

Diagram **NOT** drawn accurately

The cuboid has a base of length $2x$ and a height of $16x$.

The cuboid is melted down and made into a cube of side length s.

Find an expression for s in terms of x.
Give your answer in its simplest form.

$s^3 = 2x \times 2x \times 16x$
$= 64x^3$ ✓
$s = \sqrt[3]{64x^3}$ ✓
$= 4x$

> Write an expression for the volume of the cuboid. The volume of the cube is the same so take cube roots to find an expression for the length of one side.

$\sqrt[3]{64x^3} = \sqrt[3]{64} \times \sqrt[3]{x^3}$
Try and learn the cubes of 2, 3, 4, 5 and 10 and their corresponding cube roots.

$s = 4x$ ✓

(Total for Question 16 is 3 marks)

75

17 Work out $\dfrac{1.8 \times 10^2}{2.4 \times 10^{-3}}$

Give your answer in standard form.

$(1.8 \times 10^2) \div (2.4 \times 10^{-3}) = 75000$ ✓

> Use the $\boxed{\times 10^x}$ key on your calculator to work out the answer. Remember to write your final answer in standard form.

7.5×10^4 ✓

(Total for Question 17 is 2 marks)

---

18 The area of a trapezium is given by the formula

$$A = \frac{ah + bh}{2}$$

Rearrange this formula to make a the subject of the formula.

$2A = ah + bh$ ✓
$2A - bh = ah$ ✓
$\dfrac{2A - bh}{h} = a$

> You need to get a on its own on one side of the formula:
> - multiply both sides by 2
> - subtract bh from both sides
> - divide both sides by h.

> It doesn't matter if a ends up on the right-hand side.

$a = \dfrac{2A - bh}{h}$ ✓

(Total for Question 18 is 3 marks)

---

19 A wheelchair ramp is to be built alongside 5 steps, as shown in the diagram.

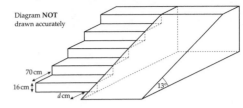

Diagram **NOT** drawn accurately

70 cm
16 cm
d cm
13°

The height of each step is 16 cm.
The depth of each step is 70 cm.
The angle of the wheelchair ramp is 13° to the horizontal.

Calculate d, the distance from the bottom of the step to where the ramp should start.
Give your answer correct to 1 decimal place.

$5 \times 16 = 80$ ✓

> The ramp needs to be $5 \times 16 = 80$ cm high.

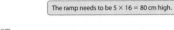

80 cm
OPP
13°
x cm
ADJ

> Sketch any right-angled triangles if you need to use trigonometry.

$\tan 13° = \dfrac{80}{x}$ ✓

$x = \dfrac{80}{\tan 13°}$ ✓

$= 346.5180...$

> $\tan x = \dfrac{\text{OPP}}{\text{ADJ}}$
> Make sure your calculator is in degrees mode.

$4 \times 70 = 280$
$346.5180... - 280 = 66.5180...$ ✓

> In the diagram the triangle only starts at the end of the top step, so you need to subtract the length of 4 steps.

66.5 ✓ cm

(Total for Question 19 is 5 marks)

---

20 Prove that the recurring decimal $0.9\dot{2}\dot{8}$ can be written as $\dfrac{919}{990}$

You must show your working.

$x = 0.928282828...$
$1000x = 928.2828...$ ✓
$-10x = 9.2828...$
$\overline{990x = 919}$ ✓
$x = \dfrac{919}{990}$ ✓

> Write out more of the recurring decimal and write it as x. You need to eliminate the recurring part, so subtract $10x$ from $1000x$, then divide both sides by 990.

(Total for Question 20 is 3 marks)

---

21 ABC is a right-angled triangle.

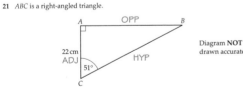

A OPP B
22 cm ADJ HYP
51°
C

Diagram **NOT** drawn accurately

Angle $ACB = 51°$.
$AC = 22$ cm.

Calculate the length of AB.
Give your answer correct to 1 decimal place.

SOH CAH (TOA)

$\tan 51° = \dfrac{AB}{22}$ ✓

$AB = 22 \times \tan 51°$ ✓
$= 27.1677...$

> You can write SOH CAH TOA to help you remember the trigonometric ratios.

> When using trigonometry in right-angled triangles, make sure you label the sides relative to the angle you are interested in.

27.2 ✓ cm

(Total for Question 21 is 3 marks)

---

22 A factory produces vending machines that dispense cups of coffee.

Two vending machines, A and B, are tested.
Each cup of coffee should contain 250 ml of hot water.

Here is some information about the amounts of hot water contained in a sample of cups from vending machine A.

Minimum	Lower quartile	Median	Upper quartile	Maximum
248	251	254	255	262

(a) Draw a box plot to represent this information.

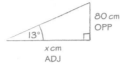

245 250 255 260 265
Amount of hot water (millilitres)

> Use a ruler and a sharp pencil.

(2)

The box plot below shows information about a sample of cups from vending machine B.

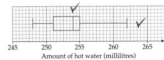

245 250 255 260 265
Amount of hot water (millilitres)

(b) Compare the distribution of amounts of hot water from vending machine A with the distribution of amounts of hot water from vending machine B.

The median for machine A (254 ml) is smaller than the median for machine B (255 ml). ✓

A: $262 - 248 = 14$ ml

B: $263 - 246 = 17$ ml

The range for machine B is greater than the range for machine A. ✓

> Compare one data point (like the median, the upper or lower quartile, or the maximum or minimum value) and one measure of spread (the range or the interquartile range).

(2)

(Total for Question 22 is 4 marks)

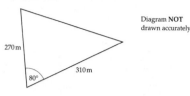

23 The diagram shows a farmer's field.

Diagram **NOT**
drawn accurately

270 m

310 m

80°

The lengths of the sides of the field have been measured to the nearest 10 m.

The farmer wants to plant grass in the field.

1 bag of seed covers 500 m², to the nearest 100 m².
The farmer has 90 bags of grass seed.

Does the farmer definitely have enough bags?
Show all your working.

	270 m	310 m	500 m²
LB	265	305	450
UB	275	315	550

✓✓

Area $= \frac{1}{2} \times 275 \times 315 \times \sin 80°$ ✓

$= 42654.4858... \text{m}^2$

$42654.4858... \div 450 = 94.7877...$ ✓

No. The farmer might need 95 bags. ✓

This is an upper and lower bounds question. Write out the upper and lower bounds for each value before you do any calculations.

To work out whether the farmer definitely has enough bags you need to consider the worst-case scenario: the upper bounds for the lengths of the sides of the field, and the lower bound for the area covered by 1 bag.

(Total for Question 23 is 5 marks)

80

24 The table shows the heights of some seedlings.

Height of seedlings, s (cm)	Frequency	Class width	Frequency density
$0 < s \le 2$	6	2	$6 \div 2 = 3$
$2 < s \le 4$	7	2	$7 \div 2 = 3.5$
$4 < s \le 6$	13	2	$13 \div 2 = 6.5$
$6 < s \le 9$	12	3	$12 \div 3 = 4$
$9 < s \le 15$	15	6	$15 \div 6 = 2.5$

Add columns to the table for class width and frequency density:
Frequency density $= \frac{\text{Frequency}}{\text{Class width}}$

Draw a histogram for this data.

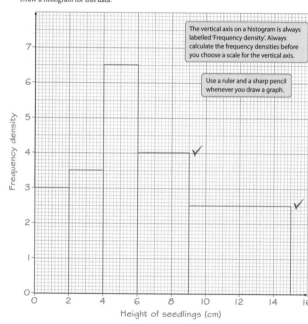

The vertical axis on a histogram is always labelled 'Frequency density'. Always calculate the frequency densities before you choose a scale for the vertical axis.

Use a ruler and a sharp pencil whenever you draw a graph.

(Total for Question 24 is 3 marks)

81

25 A secondary school has 972 students altogether.
The table shows the number of students in each year group.

Year group	7	8	9	10	11
Number of students	198	204	214	180	176

A stratified sample of 97 students is required.

Complete the table below to show how many students from each year group should be in the sample.

Year group	7	8	9	10	11	Total
Number of students	198	204	214	180	176	972
Number in sample	20	20	21	18	18	97

✓

The sampling fraction is $\frac{97}{972}$. Multiply the number of students in each year group by the sampling fraction to work out the number of students from that year group in the sample.

$198 \times \frac{97}{972} = 19.7592...$

So there should be 20 Year 7 students in the sample.

Check that there are 97 students in the sample in total.

(Total for Question 25 is 3 marks)

26 Solve $3x^2 + 5x - 4 = 0$
Give your solutions correct to 3 significant figures.

$a = 3, b = 5, c = -4$

$x = \dfrac{-5 \pm \sqrt{5^2 - 4 \times 3 \times (-4)}}{2 \times 3}$ ✓

$= \dfrac{-5 \pm \sqrt{25 + 48}}{6}$

$x = \dfrac{-5 \pm \sqrt{73}}{6}$ ✓

$= \dfrac{-5 + 8.5440...}{6}$ or $\dfrac{-5 - 8.5440...}{6}$

$= 0.5906...$ or $-2.2573...$

$x = 0.591$ or $x = -2.26$ ✓

The quadratic formula is given on the formula sheet. You can use it to solve quadratic equations on your calculator paper:
$x = \dfrac{-b \pm \sqrt{b^2 - 4ac}}{2a}$
Write down the values of a, b and c before you substitute.

(Total for Question 26 is 3 marks)

82

27

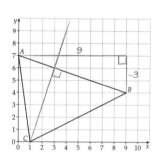

ABC is a triangle.

Work out the equation of the straight line from C which is perpendicular to AB.

Gradient of $AB = \dfrac{-3}{9} = -\dfrac{1}{3}$ ✓

$-\dfrac{1}{\left(-\dfrac{1}{3}\right)} = 3$ ✓

If a line has a gradient of m then a perpendicular line will have a gradient of $-\dfrac{1}{m}$.
The gradient of AB is $-\dfrac{1}{3}$ so the gradient of a line perpendicular to AB is 3.

$y = 3x + c$

$0 = 3 \times 1 + c$ ✓

$c = -3$

The line has gradient 3 and passes through (1, 0).
Substitute $x = 1$, $y = 0$ into $y = 3x + c$ to work out the value of c.

$y = 3x - 3$ ✓

(Total for Question 27 is 4 marks)

83

146

28

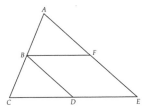

The diagram shows triangle *ACE*.

BDEF is a parallelogram where

   B is the midpoint of *AC*
   D is the midpoint of *CE*
   F is the midpoint of *AE*.

Prove that triangle *ABF* and triangle *BCD* are congruent.
You must give a reason for each stage of your proof.

$AB = CB$
B is midpoint of *AC* ✔

$AF = FE$
F is midpoint of *AE*
$BD = FE$
Opposite sides of parallelogram
So $AF = BD$ ✔

$CD = DE$
D is midpoint of *CE*
$DE = BF$
Opposite sides of parallelogram
So $CD = BF$

So *ABF* and *BCD* are congruent using SSS. ✔

> This is a proof question so you need to show all your working. You can only use the information given in the question in your proof.

> You need to state which condition of congruence you are using:
> • SSS: three sides equal
> • SAS: two sides and the included angle equal
> • AAS: two angles and a corresponding side equal
> • RHS: right angle, hypotenuse and one other side equal.

(Total for Question 28 is 3 marks)

29 Work out the *x*-coordinates of the points of intersection of

   the straight line $y = x + 4$

   the circle $x^2 + y^2 = 21$

$x^2 + (x + 4)^2 = 21$ ✔
$x^2 + x^2 + 8x + 16 = 21$ ✔
$2x^2 + 8x - 5 = 0$ ✔

$a = 2, b = 8, c = -5$
$x = \dfrac{-8 \pm \sqrt{8^2 - 4 \times 2 \times (-5)}}{2 \times 2}$ ✔

$= \dfrac{-8 \pm \sqrt{104}}{4}$

$= \dfrac{-8 + 10.1980}{4}$ or $\dfrac{-8 - 10.1980}{4}$

$x = 0.5495...$ or $-4.5495...$

> Solve the equations simultaneously using substitution.

> Use the quadratic formula. Write down the values of *a*, *b* and *c* before you substitute.

> Leave your answers as surds or give them to 3 significant figures.

$x = \underline{\quad 0.550 \quad}$
$x = \underline{\quad -4.55 \quad}$ ✔
(Total for Question 29 is 5 marks)

TOTAL FOR PAPER IS 100 MARKS

1 Terri mixed 300 g of rice with 240 g of fish.

She added some onion to the mixture.

The ratio of the weight of fish to the weight of onion was 3 : 2

Work out the ratio of the weight of rice to the weight of onion.

$240 \div 3 = 80$ ✓

$2 \times 80 = 160$ ✓

Rice : Onion = 3̶0̶0̶ : 1̶6̶0̶ = 15 : 8

> 3 parts of the ratio represent 240 g so 1 part represents 80 g. Multiply 80 g by 2 to work out the weight of onion in the dish. Then write the ratio of rice to onion and simplify it as much as possible.

$$15 : 8 \checkmark$$

(Total for Question 1 is 3 marks)

2 (a) Expand and simplify $5(m - 4) + 2(3m + 1)$

> Multiply out the brackets and then simplify the expression by collecting like terms.

$5m - 20 + 6m + 2 = 5m + 6m - 20 + 2$ ✓

$= 11m - 18$

$$11m - 18 \checkmark$$

(2)

(b) Expand $(p - q)^2$

$(p - q)(p - q) = p^2 - pq - qp + q^2$ ✓

$= p^2 - 2pq + q^2$

> Remember that $pq = qp$ and that $-q \times -q = +q^2$.

$$p^2 - 2pq + q^2 \checkmark$$

(2)

(c) Solve $5x + 2 = 3(x - 1) - 3$

$5x + 2 = 3x - 3 - 3$

$5x + 2 = 3x - 6$

$5x = 3x - 8$

$2x = -8$ ✓

$x = -4$

> Follow these steps to solve the equation:
> • multiply out the brackets
> • collect like terms
> • subtract 2 from both sides
> • subtract $3x$ from both sides
> • divide both sides by 2.

$$x = -4 \checkmark$$

(2)

(Total for Question 2 is 6 marks)

---

3 On the grid, draw the graph of $y = 2x + 3$ for values of x from -3 to 2

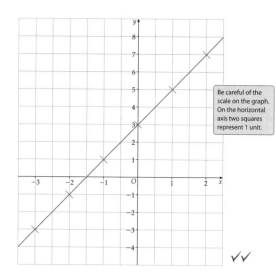

> Be careful of the scale on the graph. On the horizontal axis two squares represent 1 unit.

✓✓

x	-3	-2	-1	0	1	2
y	-3	-1	1	3	5	7

✓

> You can also use $y = mx + c$ to draw the graph. $m = 2$ so the gradient of the graph is 2. $c = 3$ so the graph crosses the y-axis at $(0, 3)$.

> Use the equation $y = 2x + 3$ to work out at least 3 pairs of coordinates. For example, when $x = -3$, $y = 2 \times (-3) + 3 = -6 + 3 = -3$

(Total for Question 3 is 3 marks)

4

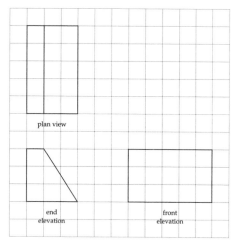

plan view

end elevation

front elevation

The diagram shows the plan view, end elevation and front elevation of a prism.
The diagram is drawn on a grid of centimetre squares.

Sketch the prism.
Show the dimensions on your diagram.

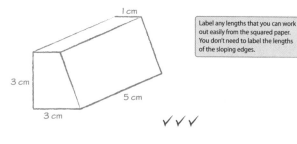

1 cm

3 cm

5 cm

3 cm

✓✓✓

> Label any lengths that you can work out easily from the squared paper. You don't need to label the lengths of the sloping edges.

(Total for Question 4 is 3 marks)

---

5 The diagram shows an enlarged square photo inside a rectangular picture frame.

40 cm

5 cm

Diagram **NOT** drawn accurately

30 cm   PHOTO

5 cm

The original square photo has a side length of 8 cm.

Work out the scale factor used to enlarge the photo.

$30 - 5 - 5 = 20$ ✓

$\dfrac{20}{8} = \dfrac{5}{2} = 2.5$ ✓

> Scale factor = $\dfrac{\text{New side length}}{\text{Original side length}}$

$$2.5 \checkmark$$

(Total for Question 5 is 3 marks)

*6 Two telephone companies offer these rates for the first 12 months of a contract.

YourTel	FastCom
£15 per month	£16 per month
Last month free	15% discount for the first 6 months

Which company is cheaper for the first 12 months?

YourTel

$11 \times 15 = 165$ ✓

FastCom

$12 \times 16 = 192$

10% of $16 = 1.6$

5% of $16 = 0.8$

15% of $16 = 2.4$ ✓

$6 \times 2.4 = 14.4$

YourTel is cheaper. ✓

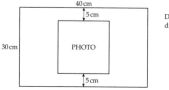

> You can work out the cost for FastCom by calculating the total cost $(12 \times £16)$ and then subtracting the discount.

> $12 \times 16 = 12 \times 10 + 12 \times 6$
> $= 120 + 72$
> $= 192$

> You can work out 6×2.4 using partitioning:
> $6 \times 2 = 12$
> $6 \times 0.4 = 6 \times 4 \div 10 = 24 \div 10 = 2.4$
> $6 \times 2.4 = 12 + 2.4 = 14.4$

(Total for Question 6 is 4 marks)

7 The diagram shows a heptagon.

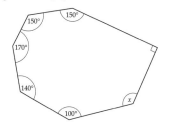

Diagram **NOT**
drawn accurately

Work out the size of angle x.

$5 \times 180 = 900$ ✓

```
    90
   150
   150
   170
   140
+  100
  ─────
   800   ✓
  ───
   3
```

$900 - 800 = 100$

The sum of the interior angles of an
n-sided polygon is $(n - 2) \times 180°$.

.... 100 ✓ °

(Total for Question 7 is 3 marks)

8 The scatter graph shows information about the numbers of people living in blocks of flats.
It shows the number of flats in a block and the total number of people living in the block.

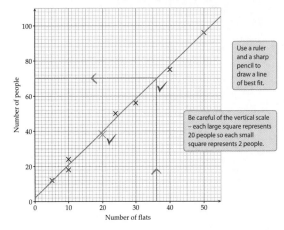

Use a ruler
and a sharp
pencil to
draw a line
of best fit.

Be careful of the vertical scale
– each large square represents
20 people so each small
square represents 2 people.

(a) What type of correlation does the scatter graph show?

.... Positive ✓

(1)

38 people live in another block of 20 flats.

(b) Plot this information on the graph.

(1)

(c) Estimate the number of people living in a block of 36 flats.

.... 70 ✓

(2)

Read up from 36 on the horizontal axis to your line of
best fit, then read across to the vertical axis. Draw lines
on your graph to show the values you are reading off.

(Total for Question 8 is 4 marks)

---

9 After dinner, Naim has to clear the table (C), wash up (W) or dry up (D).

She always spins this fair spinner to find out which task she will do.

At the weekend, Naim has two dinners.

Work out the probability that she will wash up **once** at the weekend.

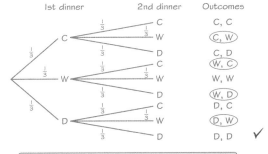

Draw a tree diagram or just list the outcomes. Each outcome has probability
$\frac{1}{3} \times \frac{1}{3} = \frac{1}{9}$, and there are 4 successful outcomes.

$P(\text{Wash up once}) = \frac{1}{9} + \frac{1}{9} + \frac{1}{9} + \frac{1}{9} = \frac{4}{9}$

.... $\frac{4}{9}$ ✓

(Total for Question 9 is 3 marks)

10 Here are the first five terms of an arithmetic sequence.

99   93   87   81   75   69 63 57 51 45 39 33 27 21 ... ✓

Marcia says that 23 is a term in this sequence.

She is wrong.
Explain why.

You could also work out the nth term
of the sequence: $105 - 6n$.
If you solve $105 - 6n = 23$ then n is not
a whole number, so 23 is not a term in
the sequence.

23 is between two terms (27 and 21) so it is not a term in the
sequence. ✓

(Total for Question 10 is 2 marks)

11 (a) Write the number 144 as a product of its prime factors.

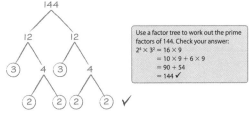

Use a factor tree to work out the prime
factors of 144. Check your answer:
$2^4 \times 3^2 = 16 \times 9$
$= 10 \times 9 + 6 \times 9$
$= 90 + 54$
$= 144$ ✓

$144 = 2 \times 2 \times 2 \times 2 \times 3 \times 3$

.... $2^4 \times 3^2$ ✓

(2)

(b) Explain why $\frac{1}{144}$ is a recurring decimal.

To check whether a fraction gives a recurring decimal:
• write it in simplest form
• work out the prime factors of its denominator
• if only prime factors are 2 and 5 → terminating
• if any other prime factors → recurring.

Its denominator (144) has prime factors other than 2 and 5. ✓

(1)

(Total for Question 11 is 3 marks)

12 Three girls shared a full bottle of cola.

Karen drank $\frac{1}{4}$ of the bottle.

Rita drank $\frac{3}{10}$ of the bottle.

Megan drank the rest.

(a) Work out the fraction of the bottle of cola which Megan drank.

$\frac{1}{4} + \frac{3}{10} = \frac{5}{20} + \frac{6}{20} = \frac{11}{20}$ ✓

$1 - \frac{11}{20} = \frac{9}{20}$ ✓

> Add up the total amount Karen and Rita drank and subtract the total from 1.

$\frac{9}{20}$ ✓
(3)

Rita drank 36 cl of cola.

(b) How much cola was in the full bottle?

$36 \div 3 = 12$

$12 \times 10 = 120$ ✓

> $\frac{3}{10}$ of the bottle was 36 cl so $\frac{1}{10}$ of the bottle was 12 cl, and the whole bottle was 120 cl. You could also work out $36 \div \frac{3}{10}$.

120 ✓ cl
(2)
(Total for Question 12 is 5 marks)

***13** These two rectangles have the same perimeter.

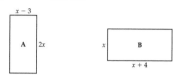

In the diagram, all of the measurements are in metres.

Work out the width and height of rectangle **A**.
Show all of your working.

<u>Rectangle A</u>

$x - 3 + x - 3 + 2x + 2x = 6x - 6$

> Work out expressions for the perimeter of each rectangle.

<u>Rectangle B</u>

$x + x + x + 4 + x + 4 = 4x + 8$

$6x - 6 = 4x + 8$ ✓
$6x = 4x + 14$
$2x = 14$
$x = 7$ ✓✓

> Write your expressions equal to each other to form an equation. Solve your equation to find x.

$x - 3 = 7 - 3 = 4$
$2x = 2 \times 7 = 14$

> Use x to work out the width and height of rectangle **A**. You need to show all of your working clearly.

width = 4 m ✓

height = 14 m ✓

(Total for Question 13 is 5 marks)

---

14 The diagram shows a pane of glass with a lead border.

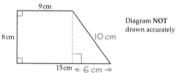

Diagram **NOT** drawn accurately

(a) Work out the area of the pane of glass.

$\frac{1}{2} \times (15 + 9) \times 8 = \frac{1}{2} \times 24 \times 8$ ✓

> Area of a trapezium = $\frac{1}{2}(a + b)h$

$= 12 \times 8$

> $12 \times 8 = 10 \times 8 + 2 \times 8 = 80 + 16 = 96$

$= 96$

96 ✓ cm^2
(2)

(b) Work out the perimeter of the pane of glass.

$15 - 9 = 6$ ✓

> Use Pythagoras' theorem to work out the length of the missing side. You can draw a right-angled triangle on the diagram, and write in any lengths you work out.

$h^2 = 6^2 + 8^2 = 36 + 64 = 100$

$h = \sqrt{100} = 10$ ✓

$8 + 9 + 10 + 15 = 42$

42 ✓ cm
(4)
(Total for Question 14 is 6 marks)

---

15 (a) Find the value of $(-5)^{-2}$

$(-5)^{-2} = \frac{1}{(-5)^2} = \frac{1}{25}$

> $(-5)^2 = (-5) \times (-5) = 25$

✓

$\frac{1}{25}$ ✓
(2)

(b) Write the reciprocal of $\sqrt{2}$ as a power of 2

$\frac{1}{\sqrt{2}} = \frac{1}{2^{\frac{1}{2}}} = 2^{-\frac{1}{2}}$

> $\sqrt{2} = 2^{\frac{1}{2}}$
> $\frac{1}{a^m} = a^{-m}$

$2^{-\frac{1}{2}}$ ✓
(2)
(Total for Question 15 is 4 marks)

---

16 (a) Factorise $8x^2 + 2x - 3$

> This is a quadratic expression, so you need to write it as the product of two brackets. It will be either:
> $(8x \pm \Box)(x \pm \Box)$
> or
> $(4x \pm \Box)(2x \pm \Box)$

$(4x + 3)(2x - 1)$ ✓✓
(2)

(b) Solve the inequality $-2 \le 3x + 7 < 13$

$-9 \le 3x < 6$ ✓

$-3 \le x < 2$

> Use inverse operations to get the variable, x, on its own. Remember, you're not allowed to multiply or divide by a negative number.

$-3 \le x < 2$ ✓
(2)

(c) Show the solutions to the inequality on the number line below.

 ✓

> Use a closed circle for $\le$ or $\ge$ and an open circle for $<$ or $>$.
(1)
(Total for Question 16 is 5 marks)

---

17 Solve the simultaneous equations

$$2x + y = 8 \quad \text{①}$$
$$5x - 3y = 31 \quad \text{②}$$

$3 \times$ ① $6x + 3y = 24$
$+$ ② $\underline{5x - 3y = 31}$
$\qquad 11x \qquad = 55$ ✓
$\qquad x \qquad = 5$

> Label the two equations first. Multiply equation ① by 3 so that the y-terms are eliminated when the equations are added.

<u>Substitute into ①</u>

$2 \times 5 + y = 8$
$10 + y = 8$
$y = -2$

<u>Check with ②</u>

$5 \times 5 - 3 \times (-2) = 25 + 6 = 31$ ✓

$x = 5$ ✓
$y = -2$ ✓
(Total for Question 17 is 3 marks)

18 A manufacturer tested 80 projector light bulbs to see how long they would last.
The cumulative frequency graph shows the results.

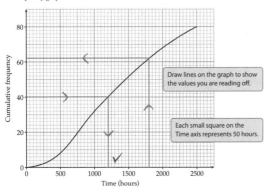

Draw lines on the graph to show the values you are reading off.

Each small square on the Time axis represents 50 hours.

(a) Estimate the median.

There were 80 data values, so read across from 40 on the vertical axis to estimate the median.

1200 ✓ .... hours
(2)

(b) Estimate the number of light bulbs that lasted more than 1800 hours.

$80 - 62 = 18$ ✓

Approximately 62 light bulbs lasted up to 1800 hours, so $80 - 62 = 18$ lasted more than 1800 hours.

18 ✓
(2)
(Total for Question 18 is 4 marks)

19 Solve the equation $(x + 2)^2 - 5(x + 2) = 0$

$x^2 + 4x + 4 - 5x - 10 = 0$
$x^2 - x - 6 = 0$ ✓
$(x + 2)(x - 3) = 0$ ✓
$x = -2$ or $x = 3$

This is a quadratic equation. Write it in the form $ax^2 + bx + c = 0$ before factorising it.

Look for two numbers which have a sum of -1 and a product of -6. They are 2 and -3.

You could also factorise the equation directly by taking a factor of $(x + 2)$ out of both terms:
$(x + 2)^2 - 5(x + 2) = 0$
$(x + 2)(x + 2 - 5) = 0$
$(x + 2)(x - 3) = 0$

$x = -2$ ✓ or $x = 3$ ✓
(Total for Question 19 is 4 marks)

20 Convert $0.35\,\mathrm{m}^3$ to mm^3, giving your answer in standard form.

$$0.35 \times 1000 \times 1000 \times 1000 = 350000000$$ ✓ ✓
$$= 3.5 \times 10^8$$

$1\,\mathrm{m}^3 = 1\,\mathrm{m} \times 1\,\mathrm{m} \times 1\,\mathrm{m}$
$= 1000\,\mathrm{mm} \times 1000\,\mathrm{mm} \times 1000\,\mathrm{mm}$
$= 1\,000\,000\,000\,\mathrm{mm}^3$

3.5×10^8 ✓ .... mm^3
(Total for Question 20 is 3 marks)

21 The speeds, in mph, of some cars were recorded as they passed a 30 mph speed limit sign.

~~42~~ ~~29~~ ~~33~~ ~~31~~ ~~27~~ ~~30~~ ~~27~~ ~~44~~
~~21~~ ~~46~~ ~~27~~ ~~46~~ ~~22~~ ~~30~~ ~~27~~

Draw a box plot for the data.

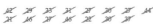
Speed (mph)   ✓ ✓

21, 22, 27, ㉗, 27, 29, 30, ㉚, 31, 33, 37, ㊷, 44, 46, 46

$\dfrac{15 + 1}{2}$ = 8th value
Median = 30 ✓

Write the data values in order of size, crossing them off the list as you go.

$\dfrac{15 + 1}{4}$ = 4th value
Lower quartile = 27 ✓

$\dfrac{3(15 + 1)}{4}$ = 12th value
Upper quartile = 42 ✓

The median is the $\dfrac{15 + 1}{2}$th value.
The lower quartile is the $\dfrac{15 + 1}{4}$th value.
The upper quartile is the $\dfrac{3(15 + 1)}{4}$th value.

(Total for Question 21 is 5 marks)

22 Rationalise the denominator of $\dfrac{12 - \sqrt{6}}{\sqrt{6}}$
Simplify your answer.

$\sqrt{6}$ is an irrational number. To rationalise the denominator you need to multiply the numerator and denominator by $\sqrt{6}$. Then simplify the fraction as much as possible.

$\dfrac{12 - \sqrt{6}}{\sqrt{6}} = \dfrac{12 - \sqrt{6}}{\sqrt{6}} \times \dfrac{\sqrt{6}}{\sqrt{6}}$

$= \dfrac{12\sqrt{6} - \sqrt{6} \times \sqrt{6}}{\sqrt{6} \times \sqrt{6}}$ ✓

$\sqrt{6} \times \sqrt{6} = 6$

$= \dfrac{12\sqrt{6} - 6}{6}$

$= 2\sqrt{6} - 1$

$2\sqrt{6} - 1$ ✓
(Total for Question 22 is 2 marks)

*23

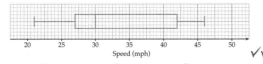

Diagram **NOT** drawn accurately

AC and BC are tangents to a circle, centre O.
Angle $ACB = 40°$.

Work out the size of angle x.
Give reasons for your answer.

$(180 - 40) \div 2 = 70$
$\angle ABC = 70°$ ✓

Base angles of an isosceles triangle are equal.

$\angle OBC = 90°$
Angle between a tangent and a radius is 90°. ✓

$90 - 70 = 20$ ✓
$x = 20°$ ✓

Triangle ABC is isosceles because tangents to a circle from a point are equal.

You could also look at the quadrilateral $AOBC$:
$\angle OBC = \angle OAC = 90°$
So $\angle AOB = 360° - 90° - 90° - 40° = 140°$
Triangle AOB is isosceles (because two of its sides are radii of the circle).
So $x = (180° - 140°) \div 2 = 20°$

(Total for Question 23 is 4 marks)

24 The diagram shows a kite *ABCD*.

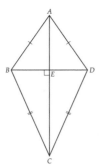

Diagram **NOT**
drawn accurately

AB = AD.
BC = DC.
Diagonals *AC* and *BD* intersect at *E*.

Prove that triangle *ABC* is congruent to triangle *ADC*.

AC is common to both triangles. ✔

AB = AD given ✔

BC = DC given ✔

Triangle ABC is congruent to triangle ADC (using SSS). ✔

> You need to state which condition of congruence you are using:
> • SSS: three sides equal
> • SAS: two sides and the included angle equal
> • AAS: two angles and a corresponding side equal
> • RHS: right angle, hypotenuse and one other side equal.

(Total for Question 24 is 3 marks)

25 A machine makes solid plastic cylinders of different heights and radii.

The height *h* cm of a plastic cylinder is inversely proportional to its radius *r* cm.

A plastic cylinder of height 6 cm has a radius of 4 cm.

Work out the height of a plastic cylinder with a radius of 3 cm.

$h = \dfrac{k}{r}$

$6 = \dfrac{k}{4}$

$k = 6 \times 4 = 24$ ✔

> Write a formula connecting *h* and *r*.
> Use the values given in the question to work out the proportionality constant, *k*.

$h = \dfrac{24}{r}$

$h = \dfrac{24}{3}$ ✔

$= 8$

> Substitute *r* = 3 into your formula to find the corresponding value of *h*.

............8............ ✔ cm

(Total for Question 25 is 3 marks)

26

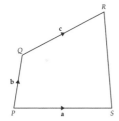

Diagram **NOT**
drawn accurately

PQRS is a quadrilateral.

$$\vec{PS} = \mathbf{a} \qquad \vec{PQ} = \mathbf{b} \qquad \vec{QR} = \mathbf{c}$$

(a) Find the vector $\vec{SR}$, in terms of **a**, **b** and **c**.

> Find a path from *S* to *R*. $\vec{PS} = \mathbf{a}$ so $\vec{SP} = -\mathbf{a}$.

$-\underline{a} + \underline{b} + \underline{c}$ ✔

(1)

$\mathbf{a} = \begin{pmatrix} 5 \\ 0 \end{pmatrix} \qquad \mathbf{b} = \begin{pmatrix} 1 \\ 3 \end{pmatrix} \qquad \mathbf{c} = \begin{pmatrix} 6 \\ 3 \end{pmatrix}$

(b) Work out the vector $\vec{SR}$.

> You can add or subtract the top numbers and bottom numbers in vectors:
> $\begin{pmatrix} a \\ b \end{pmatrix} + \begin{pmatrix} c \\ d \end{pmatrix} = \begin{pmatrix} a+c \\ b+d \end{pmatrix}$

$-\begin{pmatrix} 5 \\ 0 \end{pmatrix} + \begin{pmatrix} 1 \\ 3 \end{pmatrix} + \begin{pmatrix} 6 \\ 3 \end{pmatrix} = \begin{pmatrix} 2 \\ 6 \end{pmatrix}$

> You never simplify vectors.
> $\begin{pmatrix} 2 \\ 6 \end{pmatrix}$ is not the same vector as $\begin{pmatrix} 1 \\ 3 \end{pmatrix}$

$\begin{pmatrix} 2 \\ 6 \end{pmatrix}$ ✔

(1)

(c) What kind of quadrilateral is *PQRS*?
Give a reason for your answer.

$\vec{SR} = \begin{pmatrix} 2 \\ 6 \end{pmatrix} = 2 \times \begin{pmatrix} 1 \\ 3 \end{pmatrix} = 2 \times \vec{PQ}$ ✔

SR and PQ are parallel, so PQRS is a trapezium. ✔

(2)

(Total for Question 26 is 4 marks)

27 Here are five cards.

Each card has a different single digit printed on it.
Two of the cards have been turned over.

One of the five cards is chosen at random.

The probability that it is even is 0.4
The probability that it is **not** a square number is 0.8

Work out the two numbers on the cards which have been turned over.
Show all your working.

> Write the probability as a fraction with denominator 5. Only 2 cards are even, so the possibilities are 1, 5, 7 or 9.

$0.4 = \dfrac{2}{5}$

2 cards are even so both cards must be odd. ✔

$0.8 = \dfrac{4}{5}$

4 cards are not square numbers, so only 1 card (the 4) is a square number. ✔

> Only 1 card is a square number, so neither missing card is a square number. You can eliminate 1 and 9, so the missing cards are 5 and 7.

Missing cards are 5 and 7. ✔

(Total for Question 27 is 3 marks)

TOTAL FOR PAPER IS 100 MARKS

102

104

1 The diagram shows two types of plastic building block.

A

B

Diagram **NOT** drawn accurately

← 24 mm →

← 32 mm →

Block **A** is 24 mm long.
Block **B** is 32 mm long.

Jeremy joins some type **A** blocks together make a straight row.
He then joins some type **B** blocks together to make a straight row of the same length.

Write down the shortest possible length of this row.

> The length of the row of type **A** blocks must be a multiple of 24, and the length of the row of type **B** blocks must be a multiple of 32. The shortest possible length is the lowest common multiple (LCM) of 24 and 32.

Multiples of 24: 24, 48, 72, ⟨96⟩...

Multiples of 32: 32, 64, ⟨96⟩... ✔

.............96.... ✔........ mm

(Total for Question 21 is 2 marks)

2 (a) Factorise completely $15s^2t + 10st^2$

> $5(3s^2t + 2st^2)$ and $5s(3st + 2t^2)$ are only partly factorised.

.............$5st(3s + 2t)$.... ✔✔........

(2)

(b) Factorise completely $2(t - 3)^2 - 5(t - 3)$

$(t - 3)(2(t - 3) - 5) = (t - 3)(2t - 6 - 5)$ ✔

> You can take a factor of $(t - 3)$ out of both terms. Simplify each factor as much as possible.

.............$(t - 3)(2t - 11)$.... ✔........

(2)

(Total for Question 2 is 4 marks)

3 Alec asked a group of people how many text messages they sent yesterday.
The table shows the results.

Number	Frequency f	Midpoint x	$f \times x$
0–4	38	2	76
5–9	24	7	168
10–14	22	12	264
15–19	15	17	255
20–24	15	22	330
Total	114		1093

> Add columns to your table for 'Midpoint' and 'Frequency × Midpoint'. Add a row to your table for the Total frequency and the sum of the $f \times x$ column.

✔   ✔

Work out an estimate for the mean of the data.

$1093 \div 114 = 9.5877...$ ✔

> Estimate of the mean = $\dfrac{\text{Sum of } f \times x \text{ column}}{\text{Total frequency}}$

> Write down at least 4 decimal places of your calculator display before rounding your answer to 1 d.p.

.............9.6.... ✔........

(Total for Question 3 is 4 marks)

4 (a) Simplify $\dfrac{12a^5}{3a^3}$

> Cancel the number parts and cancel the variable parts. Use this index law: $a^m \div a^n = a^{m-n}$

.............$4a^2$.... ✔✔........

(2)

(b) Simplify $(4m^3n)^3$

$(4m^3n)^3 = 4^3m^{3\times3}n^3$ ✔

> Remember to cube every part of the term. Use this index law: $(a^m)^n = a^{m \times n}$

.............$64m^9n^3$.... ✔........

(2)

(Total for Question 4 is 4 marks)

5 (a) Calculate $\left(4 - \sqrt{\dfrac{7.2}{5}}\right)^3$

Write down all the figures on your calculator display.

$\sqrt{\dfrac{7.2}{5}} = \sqrt{1.44} = 1.2$ ✔

$(4 - 1.2)^3 = 21.952$

> If you work the calculation out in two steps, show all your working.

.............21.952.... ✔........

(2)

(b) Write your answer to part (a) correct to 1 decimal place.

> You have to write the 0 to show you have rounded to 1 decimal place.

.............22.0.... ✔........

(1)

(Total for Question 5 is 3 marks)

6 Taahir weighs each potato in a bag.
These are his results.

200 g   221 g   184 g   199 g   223 g

198 g   190 g   186 g   206 g   219 g

186 g   205 g   206 g   192 g   198 g

> Cross off each value as you enter it in your stem and leaf diagram.

(a) Complete the stem and leaf diagram for the data.

| 18 | 4   6   6 |
| 19 | 0   0   2   8   9 | ✔
| 20 | 0   5   6   6 |
| 21 | 9 |
| 22 | 1   3 | ✔

> Key:
> 18 | 4 represents 184 g ✔

> Remember to include a key, and check that you have written 15 'leaves'.

(3)

Taahir finds another potato in the bag that weighs 220 g.

(b) Has the range of weights changed?
Give a reason for your answer.

.....No, because 220 g is not the largest or the smallest value. ✔.....

(1)

(Total for Question 6 is 4 marks)

7 A bowl contains 6270 ml of drink.

David fills 10 glasses with 60 ml of drink every minute.
At the same time, Rosa fills 6 glasses with 90 ml of drink every minute.

How long will it take to empty the bowl?

$10 \times 60 = 600$

$6 \times 90 = 540$

$600 + 540 = 1140$ ✓

$6270 \div 1140 = 5.5$
✓

> Work out how much drink is used each minute.

> Divide the total amount of drink in the bowl by the total used each minute.

> Don't give answers in minutes as a decimal. Write $5\frac{1}{2}$ minutes, or 5 minutes and 30 seconds.

5 minutes and 30 seconds ✓

(Total for Question 7 is 3 marks)

8 A skateboard costs £42.25 plus 20% VAT.

Work out the cost of the skateboard.

$100 + 20 = 120$

$\frac{120}{100} = 1.2$ ✓

$42.25 \times 1.2 = 50.7$
✓

> The multiplier for a 20% increase is 1.2.

> Give answers in pounds to 2 decimal places.

£ 50.70 ✓

(Total for Question 8 is 3 marks)

9 The equation

$$\frac{x^2}{1+x} = 2$$

has a solution between 2 and 3

Use a trial improvement method to find this solution.
Give your answer correct to 1 decimal place.
You must show all your working.

x	$\dfrac{x^2}{1+x}$	Too big or too small?
2.5	1.7857...	Too small ✓
2.7	1.9702...	Too small
2.8	2.0631...	Too big
2.75	2.0166...	Too big ✓✓

> Work out $\frac{x^2}{1+x}$ for different values of x between 2 and 3. Use a table like this to keep track of your working.

> You need to try $x = 2.75$ to check whether x is closer to 2.7 or 2.8.

$x =$ 2.7 ✓

(Total for Question 9 is 4 marks)

*10 1.25 kg of a type of cheese costs €16.55 in France.
$1\frac{1}{2}$ lb of the same cheese costs £8.97 in England.

In which country is it cheaper to buy the cheese?
Show all of your working.

1 kg = 2.2 lb
£1 = €1.15

France
€16.55 ÷ 1.25 = €13.24 ✓

13.24 ÷ 1.15 = 11.5130...

1 kg costs £11.51 ✓

England
1.5 lb ÷ 2.2 = 0.6818... kg ✓

8.97 ÷ 0.6818... = 13.156

1 kg costs £13.16 ✓

It is cheaper in France. ✓

> You need to compare in the same units. Work out the cost in pounds per kg in both countries. For England you have to convert lb into kg, and for France you have to convert € into £.

(Total for Question 10 is 5 marks)

11 Liz stood next to her dog Jock.

She threw a stick 40 metres away from them.

Jock took 8 seconds to reach the stick, running at a constant speed.

He spent 2 seconds picking up the stick.

Jock ran back to Liz at a constant speed of 4 m/s.

(a) Use the grid below to draw a distance–time graph.

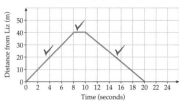

> You need to work out how long it takes Jock to run back to Liz. Draw the formula triangle for speed:
> Time = $\dfrac{\text{Distance}}{\text{Speed}}$

$T = \dfrac{D}{S} = \dfrac{40}{4} = 10$

(3)

(b) Work out Jock's speed when he was running towards the stick.
Give your answer in km/h.

$S = \dfrac{D}{T} = \dfrac{40}{8} = 5$ m/s ✓

$5 \times 60 \times 60 = 18\,000$ m/hour ✓

$18\,000 \div 1000 = 18$ km/h

> Jock's speed is 5 m/s. To convert into km/h you multiply by $60 \times 60 = 3600$ then divide by 1000.

18 ✓ km/h
(3)

(Total for Question 11 is 6 marks)

12 A goat is tied by a rope to a railing AB shown in the diagram.

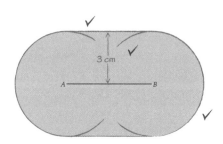

> The locus of points a fixed distance from a line segment consists of two straight lines and two semi-circles. Measure your lengths correct to the nearest mm, and don't rub out any construction lines.

The diagram is drawn using a scale of 1 cm to 1 m.

The rope is 3 m long.
The end of the rope can slide along the railing.

Make an accurate drawing to show the greatest area in which the goat can walk.

(Total for Question 12 is 3 marks)

13

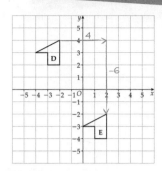

(a) Rotate shape **A** 90° anti-clockwise about the origin (0, 0).
    Label the image **B**.

(2)

(b) The line $y = -x$ is drawn on the diagram.
    Reflect the shape **B** in this line.
    Label the image **C**.

(2)

(Question 13 continued on next page)

> Use tracing paper to check a rotation:
> • trace the shape
> • put a pencil or compass point on the centre of rotation
> • rotate the tracing paper.

> Use tracing paper to check a reflection:
> • trace the shape and the mirror line
> • turn the tracing paper over and line up the mirror line.

(c) Fully describe the transformation that maps shape **D** onto shape **E**.

Translation ✓ using vector $\begin{pmatrix} 4 \\ -6 \end{pmatrix}$ ✓

(2)

> You need to write the word 'translation' and give the vector. Remember, the top number describes the horizontal movement and the bottom number describes the vertical movement.

(Total for Question 13 is 6 marks)

14 A straight line has the equation $y = 4x - 3$

> Compare the equation of the graph with $y = mx + c$. m is the gradient.

(a) Write down the gradient of the line.

4 ✓

(1)

(b) Write down the equation of another straight line that is perpendicular to the line with equation $y = 4x - 3$

> If a line has gradient m, then a perpendicular line has gradient $-\frac{1}{m}$.

> You can write $y = -\frac{1}{4}x \pm$ anything

$y = -\frac{1}{4}x$ ✓

(1)

(Total for Question 14 is 2 marks)

115

---

15 The Inland Revenue deduct tax each month from Ewan's earnings.

They base their calculations on Ewan's annual salary.

First they subtract his personal allowance of £8105 from his annual salary.
Next they calculate 20% of the remainder.
Then they divide this amount by 12 to get the amount of tax he pays each month.

> You need to work backwards through these calculations.

Ewan pays tax of £224 each month.

Work out his annual salary.

$224 \times 12 = 2688$ ✓

> Ewan pays £2688 tax per year.

$2688 \times 5 = 13\,440$ ✓

> £2688 is 20%. Multiply by 5 to work out 100%.

$13\,440 + 8105 = 21\,545$
✓

> Add on Ewan's personal allowance.

£ ......21 545...... ✓

(Total for Question 15 is 4 marks)

16 The density of copper is 8.92 g/cm³.
    The density of silver is 10.49 g/cm³.

20 cm³ of copper and 5 cm³ of silver are mixed together to make a new kind of metal.

Work out the density of the new metal.

> Write out the formula triangle for density.

$M = D \times V$

$M = 8.92 \times 20 + 10.49 \times 5 = 230.85$ ✓

> The mass of the new metal is 230.85 g.

$D = \dfrac{M}{V}$

$230.85 \div 25 = 9.234$
✓

> The volume of the new metal is 20 + 5 = 25 cm³.

......9.234...... ✓ g/cm³

(Total for Question 16 is 3 marks)

17 Make v the subject of the formula $T = (n + 2v)^2$

$\sqrt{T} = n + 2v$ ✓

$\sqrt{T} - n = 2v$ ✓

$\dfrac{\sqrt{T} - n}{2} = v$

> Use inverse operations to get v on its own on one side of the formula. Be careful with your square roots. $\sqrt{T} - n$ is not the same as $\sqrt{T - n}$.

$v = \dfrac{\sqrt{T} - n}{2}$ ✓

(Total for Question 17 is 3 marks)

18 $R = \dfrac{V}{I}$

$V = 2000$
$I = 5.2 \times 10^{-5}$

Work out the value of R.
Give your answer in standard form, correct to 2 significant figures.

$R = 2000 \div (5.2 \times 10^{-5})$

$= 38461538.46...$ ✓

$= 38000000$ (2 s.f.)

> Use the $\boxed{\times 10^x}$ key on your calculator to work out the answer. Remember to write your final answer in standard form.

3.8×10^7 ✓

(Total for Question 18 is 2 marks)

117

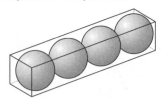

19 The diagram shows four metal ball bearings of diameter 2.7 cm packed inside the smallest possible box in the shape of a cuboid.

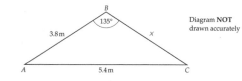

Diagram **NOT** drawn accurately

Work out the volume of empty space inside the box.
Give your answer correct to 3 significant figures.

Spheres

$2.7 \div 2 = 1.35$

> The volume of a sphere is given on the formula sheet. It is $\frac{4}{3}\pi r^3$. Convert diameter into radius by dividing by 2.

$\frac{4}{3}\pi \times (1.35)^3 = 10.3059947...$ ✓

$4 \times 10.3059947... = 41.2239788...$

Cuboid

$4 \times 2.7 = 10.8$

$2.7 \times 2.7 \times 10.8 = 78.732$ ✓

> The spheres just fit inside the cuboid, so it has a length of $4 \times 2.7 = 10.8$ cm and a width and height of 2.7 cm.

$78.732 - 41.2239788... = 37.5080212...$ ✓

> Don't round any values until the end of your calculation.

<u>   37.5   ✓   </u> cm³

(Total for Question 19 is 4 marks)

20

B

135°

x

3.8 m

Diagram **NOT** drawn accurately

A 5.4 m C

ABC is a triangle.

$AC = 5.4$ m.
$AB = 3.8$ m.
Angle $ABC = 135°$.

Calculate the length of *BC*.
Give your answer correct to 2 decimal places.

> The sine rule is given on the formula sheet. You can use it for any triangle when you know a side and the opposite angle.

$\frac{\sin C}{3.8} = \frac{\sin 135°}{5.4}$ ✓

> Use this version of the sine rule to find a missing angle:
> $\frac{\sin A}{a} = \frac{\sin B}{b} = \frac{\sin C}{c}$

$\sin C = \frac{3.8 \times \sin 135°}{5.4}$

$= 0.4975...$

$C = 29.8409...°$ ✓

$180 - 135 - 29.8409... = 15.1590...°$ ✓

$\frac{x}{\sin 15.1590...°} = \frac{5.4}{\sin 135°}$ ✓

> Use this version of the sine rule to find a missing side:
> $\frac{a}{\sin A} = \frac{b}{\sin B} = \frac{c}{\sin C}$

$x = \frac{5.4 \times \sin 15.1590...°}{\sin 135°}$

> You could also use the cosine rule to find *BC*.

$= 1.9970...$

<u>   2.00   ✓   </u> cm

(Total for Question 20 is 5 marks)

21 Carla is investigating how much time retired people spend watching TV.

She wants to choose a random sample of 40 retired people living in her town of Ashbury, stratified by age and gender.

The table shows information about the numbers of retired people in Ashbury.

	Age (years)		
	65–74	**75–84**	**85 and above**
Male	2000	800	400
Female	2400	1600	800

(a) How many females in the age range 75–84 should be in Carla's sample?

$2000 + 800 + 400 + 2400 + 1600 + 800 = 8000$

$\frac{1600}{8000} \times 40 = 8$

> There were 8000 retired people living in Ashbury in total.

✓

<u>   8   ✓   </u>

(2)

(b) Describe how Carla should choose a random sample.

Number the 1600 females from 1 to 1600 and choose 8 numbers at random using a computer. ✓

(1)

Carla wants to give each person in the sample a questionnaire.

(c) Write a suitable question she could use to find out how much time they spend watching TV.

Roughly how much time do you spend watching TV each day? ✓

☐ None
☐ Less than 1 hour
☐ From 1 hour to less than 2 hours
☐ From 2 hours to less than 3 hours
☐ 3 or more hours ✓

> Make sure your question includes a time frame, like 'each day' or 'each week'.

> Include response boxes and make sure they don't overlap.

(2)

(Total for Question 21 is 5 marks)

22 Cayden weighed 60 filled shopping bags at the checkout counter of a supermarket.
She drew this histogram for the data.

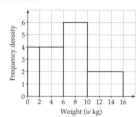

> Look at where each bar starts and ends to work out the class intervals.

Complete the frequency table.

> Frequency density $= \frac{\text{Frequency}}{\text{Class width}}$
>
> Frequency = Frequency density × Class width

Weight (*w* kg)	Frequency
$0 < w \leq 2$	$4 \times 2 = 8$ ✓
$2 < w \leq 6$	$4 \times 4 = 16$
$6 < w \leq 10$	$6 \times 4 = 24$
$10 < w \leq 16$ ✓	$2 \times 6 = 12$ ✓

(Total for Question 22 is 3 marks)

*23 Prove using algebra that the product of two odd numbers is an odd number.

$$(2m + 1)(2n + 1) = 4mn + 2m + 2n + 1 \checkmark$$
$$= 2(2mn + m + n) + 1 \checkmark$$

> Use $2n + 1$ to represent an odd number using algebra. You can represent a different odd number as $2m + 1$.

Since m and n are whole numbers, $2mn + m + n$ is a whole number, so $2(2mn + m + n) + 1$ is odd.

> You need to show that $(2m + 1)(2n + 1)$ is an odd number. To do this you need to show that you can write it as $2k + 1$ where k is a whole number.

(Total for Question 23 is 3 marks)

24 Solve $2x^2 - 10x + 5 = 0$
Give your solutions correct to 3 significant figures.

$$a = 2, \ b = -10, \ c = 5$$
$$x = \frac{-(-10) \pm \sqrt{(-10)^2 - 4 \times 2 \times 5}}{2 \times 2} \checkmark$$
$$= \frac{10 \pm \sqrt{100 - 40}}{4}$$
$$= \frac{10 \pm \sqrt{60}}{4} \checkmark$$
$$= \frac{10 + 7.7459...}{4} \ \text{ or } \ \frac{10 - 7.7459...}{4}$$
$$= 4.4364... \ \text{ or } \ 0.5635...$$

> The quadratic formula is given on the formula sheet. You can use it to solve quadratic equations on your calculator paper:
> $x = \frac{-b \pm \sqrt{b^2 - 4ac}}{2a}$
> Write down the values of a, b and c before you substitute.

$x = 4.44$ or 0.564 $\checkmark$

(Total for Question 24 is 3 marks)

25 (a) Complete the table of values for $y = 2^x$

x	-1	0	1	2	3	4
y	$\frac{1}{2}$	1	2	4	8	16

> Remember that $a^0 = 1$ for any number, a.

(2)

(b) On the grid, draw the graph of $y = 2^x$ for values of x from -1 to 4

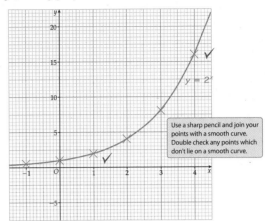

> Use a sharp pencil and join your points with a smooth curve. Double check any points which don't lie on a smooth curve.

(2)

(Total for Question 25 is 4 marks)

26 The shaded part of the diagram shows a segment of a circle, centre O.

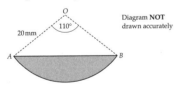

Diagram **NOT** drawn accurately

Points A and B lie on the circumference.
Angle $AOB = 110°$.
$OA = 20$ mm.

Work out the area of the segment.
Give your answer to the nearest mm².

> Subtract the area of the triangle from the area of the whole sector to work out the area of the shaded segment.

$$\frac{110}{360} \times \pi \times 20^2 = \frac{1100}{9}\pi \ \checkmark$$

$$0.5 \times 20 \times 20 \times \sin 110° = 187.9385... \ \checkmark$$

> Don't round any values until the end of your calculation. You can write down at least 4 decimal places from your calculator display, or leave answers in terms of π.

$$\frac{1100}{9}\pi - 187.9385... = 196.0339...$$
$$\checkmark$$

196 $\checkmark$ mm²

(Total for Question 26 is 4 marks)

27 The probability that a student at Jen's school has a dog is 0.3
If a student has a dog, the probability that they have a cat is 0.12
If a student does not have a dog, the probability that they have a cat is 0.25

A student is chosen at random.
Work out the probability that they do **not** have a cat.

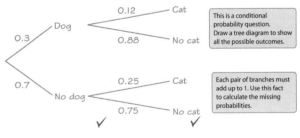

> This is a conditional probability question. Draw a tree diagram to show all the possible outcomes.

> Each pair of branches must add up to 1. Use this fact to calculate the missing probabilities.

$$0.3 \times 0.88 + 0.7 \times 0.75 = 0.264 + 0.525 = 0.789$$
$$\checkmark$$

> You are interested in two outcomes:
> • P(Dog, No cat) = 0.3 × 0.88
> • P(No dog, No cat) = 0.7 × 0.75

0.789 $\checkmark$

(Total for Question 27 is 4 marks)

TOTAL FOR PAPER IS 100 MARKS